**KT-442-677**

Computational Thinking

Computational thinking is all about the steps you take to find the best solution to a complex problem. To be honest, your decision to buy this revision guide shows that you're already a great computational thinker.

Three Key Techniques for Computational Thinking

DECOMPOSITION — breaking a complex problem down into smaller problems and solving each one individually.

Computational Thinking

ABSTRACTION — picking out the important bits of information from the problem, ignoring the specific details that don't matter.

ALGORITHMIC THINKING — a logical way of getting from the problem to the solution. If the steps you take to solve a problem follow an algorithm then they can be reused and adapted to solve similar problems in the future.

Don't worry, algorithm to the vets

These techniques are all used in Real-Life...

Computational thinking is something you'll do all the time without even noticing.

For example, when deciding which film to watch at the cinema with your family:

Decomposition	Abstraction	
Things to look at	Details to ignore	Details to focus on
What type of films are on?	Plot details, actors and director.	Film genre and age rating.
What times are the films on?	Days other than the date you're going.	Start and end times on the date you're going.
What are the reviews like?	In depth analysis of the characters and plot.	Ratings

Algorithmic thinking may involve coming up with some logical steps to reach a decision.
E.g. listing all of the films that are showing, then deleting all the age restricted films and ones with poor ratings. Getting each family member to vote for their favourite, then picking the film with the most votes.

If the family went to see a film the following week they could use the same processes of decomposition, abstraction and algorithmic thinking, but they would have to do the research and make the decisions again.

... and the Same Skills can be used in Computer Science

Computer scientists rely on decomposition, abstraction and algorithmic thinking to help them turn a complex problem into small problems that a computer can help them to solve.

See p5-6 for more on sorting algorithms.

Imagine the task is to sort a list of product names into alphabetical order:

- One part of the decomposition might decide what alphabetical order means — letters are straightforward but what if some entries in the list contain numbers and punctuation?

- Another part of the decomposition might look at comparing the entries — this could be decomposed further into how you could compare two entries, three entries, etc.

- Abstraction will help the programmer focus on the important bits — it doesn't matter what the entries are and what they mean. The important information is the order of the characters in each entry.

- Algorithmic thinking will put the tasks into a step by step process. For example, you might compare the first two entries and order them, then compare the third entry to each of the first two and put it in the correct place, then compare the fourth entry to each of the first three, etc.

I wasn't picking my nose, I was just doing a bit of abstraction...

Decomposition and abstraction are important skills that you'll need to develop if you want to succeed in your exams. You should be able to take a problem, break it down into small manageable tasks and ignore all of the details that don't matter. Try out your skills whenever you have a real-life decision to make.

Writing Algorithms — Pseudo-code

Algorithms are just sets of <u>instructions</u> for solving a problem. In real-life they can take the forms of recipes, assembly instructions, directions, etc. but in computer science they are often written in pseudo-code.

Algorithms can be written using Pseudo-code

1) Pseudo-code is not an actual programming language but it should follow a <u>similar structure</u> and <u>read like one</u> (roughly). The idea is that pseudo-code clearly shows an algorithm's steps without worrying about the <u>finer details</u> (syntax) of any particular programming language.

2) It is <u>quick to write</u> and can be <u>easily converted</u> into any programming language.

3) There are different ways to write pseudo-code — they are all <u>equally correct</u> as long as the person reading the code can <u>follow it</u> and <u>understand</u> what you mean.

 Write an algorithm using pseudo-code to calculate the salary of a worker after a 10% pay increase.

A <u>simple solution</u> to the problem would be:

```
Take worker's current salary
Multiply the salary by 1.1
Display the answer
```

This solution is perfectly adequate as the problem has been <u>split down</u> into steps and it is <u>obvious</u> to the reader what to do at <u>each stage</u>.

A more <u>useful solution</u> is shown here:

```
salary ← USERINPUT
newsalary ← salary * 1.1
OUTPUT newsalary
```

This solution is better as the <u>words</u> and <u>structure</u> resemble a real <u>programming language</u>. It can be more <u>easily adapted</u> into real code.

Make sure your pseudo-code isn't Too Vague

Even though pseudo-code isn't a formal <u>programming language</u> you still need to make sure it's <u>readable</u>, <u>easy to interpret</u> and not too <u>vague</u>.

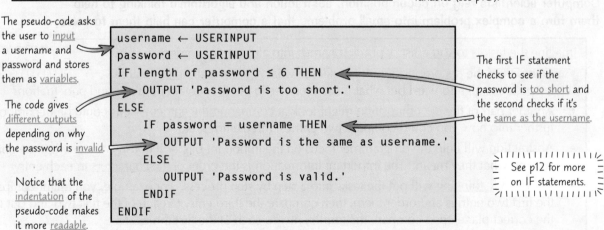

P.E.A. Fingers up Ma'am
You're coming with me.

 When registering on a website, a user's password should be more than 6 characters long and it must be different from their username. Write an algorithm to check if the password is valid. If it's invalid it should say why.

```
IF the length of the password is less than or equal
to 6 characters long OR password is the same as the
username THEN it is invalid ELSE the password is valid
```

This code is <u>too vague</u> and <u>unstructured</u>. It won't give reasons why the password is invalid and doesn't give any input variables (see p10).

The pseudo-code asks the user to <u>input</u> a username and password and stores them as <u>variables</u>.

The code gives <u>different outputs</u> depending on why the password is <u>invalid</u>.

Notice that the <u>indentation</u> of the pseudo-code makes it more <u>readable</u>.

```
username ← USERINPUT
password ← USERINPUT
IF length of password ≤ 6 THEN
    OUTPUT 'Password is too short.'
ELSE
    IF password = username THEN
        OUTPUT 'Password is the same as username.'
    ELSE
        OUTPUT 'Password is valid.'
    ENDIF
ENDIF
```

The first IF statement checks to see if the password is <u>too short</u> and the second checks if it's the <u>same as the username</u>.

See p12 for more on IF statements.

Pseudo-code isn't always everything it appears to be...

An algorithm is not that same thing as a computer program. A computer program is just one possible implementation of the algorithm — there are often many different ways to implement the same algorithm.

Writing Algorithms — Flowcharts

Algorithms can also be shown using a flowchart, and just like for pseudo-code, there are different ways to write the same algorithm. You do get to draw some different shapes though, so things are looking up.

Flowcharts use Different Boxes for different Commands

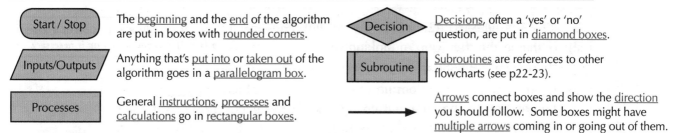

Start / Stop — The <u>beginning</u> and the <u>end</u> of the algorithm are put in boxes with <u>rounded corners</u>.

Inputs/Outputs — Anything that's <u>put into</u> or <u>taken out</u> of the algorithm goes in a <u>parallelogram box</u>.

Processes — General <u>instructions</u>, <u>processes</u> and <u>calculations</u> go in <u>rectangular boxes</u>.

Decision — <u>Decisions</u>, often a 'yes' or 'no' question, are put in <u>diamond boxes</u>.

Subroutine — <u>Subroutines</u> are references to other flowcharts (see p22-23).

<u>Arrows</u> connect boxes and show the <u>direction</u> you should follow. Some boxes might have <u>multiple arrows</u> coming in or going out of them.

Algorithms can be written as Flowcharts

Flowcharts can show <u>sequences</u>, <u>selections</u>, <u>iterations</u> or a combination of them.

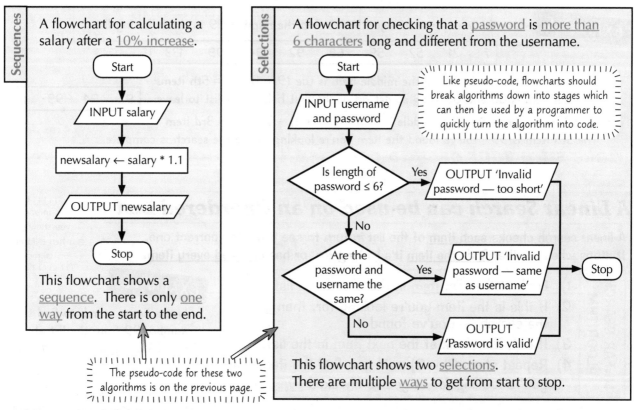

Sequences

A flowchart for calculating a salary after a <u>10% increase</u>.

Start
↓
INPUT salary
↓
newsalary ← salary * 1.1
↓
OUTPUT newsalary
↓
Stop

This flowchart shows a <u>sequence</u>. There is only <u>one way</u> from the start to the end.

The pseudo-code for these two algorithms is on the previous page.

Selections

A flowchart for checking that a <u>password</u> is <u>more than 6 characters</u> long and different from the username.

Start
↓
INPUT username and password
↓
Is length of password ≤ 6? — Yes → OUTPUT 'Invalid password — too short'
↓ No
Are the password and username the same? — Yes → OUTPUT 'Invalid password — same as username' → Stop
↓ No
OUTPUT 'Password is valid'

Like pseudo-code, flowcharts should break algorithms down into stages which can then be used by a programmer to quickly turn the algorithm into code.

This flowchart shows two <u>selections</u>. There are multiple <u>ways</u> to get from start to stop.

Iterations

A flowchart for a <u>linear search</u> (see p4).

Start → Are there more items to search? — No → OUTPUT 'Item not found' → Stop
Are there more items to search? — Yes → Check next item → Is this the right item? — Yes → OUTPUT 'Item found' → Stop
Is this the right item? — No → (back to Are there more items to search?)

This flowchart shows an <u>iteration</u> — it contains a <u>loop</u> that allows you to repeat a task.

Check out my flow, as the words just go, to and fro, yo...

Flowcharts should show the general flow of an algorithm without going into too much detail at each step. When you're making your own flowchart, make sure that all paths lead to the end. My best friend once got stuck in a flowchart — he got caught up in an infinite loop and was never seen again...

Search Algorithms

Computers need to follow search algorithms to find items in a list — the ones you'll need to know about are binary search and linear search. Now, if only someone could make a search algorithm to find my keys.

A Binary Search looks for items in an Ordered List

BINARY SEARCH ALGORITHM

1) Find the <u>middle item</u> in the ordered list.
2) If this is the item you're looking for, then <u>stop</u> the search — you've found it.
3) If not, <u>compare</u> the item you're <u>looking for</u> to the <u>middle item</u>. If it comes <u>before</u> the middle item, get rid of the <u>second half</u> of the list. If it comes <u>after</u> the middle item, get rid of the <u>first half</u> of the list.
4) You'll be left with a list that is <u>half the size</u> of the original list. Repeat steps 1) – 3) on this <u>smaller list</u> to get an even smaller one. Keep going until you find the item you're looking for.

To find the <u>middle item</u> in a list of n items do (n + 1) ÷ 2 and round up if necessary.

OK, so get rid of all the teeth on the left...

EXAMPLE: Use the binary search algorithm to find the number 99 in the following list.

| 7 | 21 | 52 | 59 | 68 | 92 | 94 | 99 | 133 |

There are 9 items in the list so the middle item is the (9 + 1) ÷ 2 = 5th item.
The 5th item is 68 and 68 < <u>99</u> so get rid of the first half of the list to leave:

| 92 | 94 | 99 | 133 |

There are 4 items left so the middle item is the (4 + 1) ÷ 2 = 2.5 = 3rd item
The 3rd item is 99. You've found the item you're looking for so the search is complete.

A Linear Search can be used on an Unordered List

It's important that you show <u>every step</u> when following these algorithms.

A linear search checks <u>each item</u> of the list in turn to see if it's the correct one. It stops when it either <u>finds the item</u> it's looking for, or has <u>checked every item</u>.

LINEAR SEARCH ALGORITHM

1) Look at the <u>first item</u> in the unordered list.
2) If this is the item you're looking for, then <u>stop</u> the search — you've found it.
3) If not, then look at the <u>next item</u> in the list.
4) Repeat steps 2) – 3) until you find the item that you're looking for or you've checked <u>every item</u>.

1) A linear search is much <u>simpler</u> than a binary search but not as <u>efficient</u> (see p28). The biggest advantage of a linear search is that it can be used on <u>any type</u> of list, it doesn't have to be ordered.
2) For <u>small ordered lists</u> the difference in efficiency doesn't really matter so the run time of both algorithms will be <u>similar</u>.
3) For <u>large ordered lists</u> the run time of binary search will generally be <u>much quicker</u> than linear search.

EXAMPLE:

Use a linear search to find the number 99 from the list above.

Check the first item:	7 ≠ 99
Look at the next item:	21 ≠ 99
Look at the next item:	52 ≠ 99
Look at the next item:	59 ≠ 99
Look at the next item:	68 ≠ 99
Look at the next item:	92 ≠ 99
Look at the next item:	94 ≠ 99
Look at the next item:	99 = 99

You've found the item you're looking for so the search is complete.

And my search for the perfect chocolate sundae continues...

Search algorithms might seem like a bit of a faff for you to follow when you can just look at a list and pick out the item you want straight away. Sadly computers are more systematic and they need to follow specific algorithms to be able to find what they're looking for. Make sure that when you're following these search algorithms you follow every step exactly as a computer would and don't go skipping ahead.

Sorting Algorithms

I'm sure you all know how to sort things into numerical or alphabetical order but try telling a computer that. You'll need to be able to follow and carry out the two sorting algorithms on the next two pages.

A Bubble Sort compares Pairs of items

The bubble sort algorithm is used to sort an unordered list of items.
The algorithm is very simple to follow but can often take a while to actually sort a list.

BUBBLE SORT ALGORITHM

1) Look at the first two items in the list.
2) If they're in the right order, you don't have to do anything.
   If they're in the wrong order, swap them.
3) Move on to the next pair of items (the 2nd and 3rd entries) and repeat step 2).
4) Repeat step 3) until you get to the end of the list — this is called one pass.
   The last item will now be in the correct place, so don't include it in the next pass.
5) Repeat steps 1) – 4) until there are no swaps in a pass.

Each pass will have one less comparison than the one before it.

EXAMPLE:

Use the bubble sort algorithm to write these numbers in ascending order.

| 66 | 21 | 38 | 15 | 89 | 49 |

First pass:

66 21 38 15 89 49	Compare **66** and **21** — swap them.
21 66 38 15 89 49	Compare **66** and **38** — swap them.
21 38 66 15 89 49	Compare **66** and **15** — swap them.
21 38 15 66 89 49	Compare **66** and **89** — no swap.
21 38 15 66 89 49	Compare **89** and **49** — swap them.
21 38 15 66 49 89	End of first pass.

After the 2nd pass the order of the numbers will be: 21 15 38 49 66 89
After the 3rd pass the order of the numbers will be: 15 21 38 49 66 89
There are no swaps in the 4th pass so the list has been sorted: 15 21 38 49 66 89

The bubble sort is considered to be one of the simplest sorting algorithms as it only ever focuses on two items rather than the whole list of items.

Pros
- It's a simple algorithm that can be easily implemented on a computer.
- It's an efficient way to check if a list is already in order. For a list of n items you only have to do one pass of $n - 1$ comparisons to check if the list is ordered or not.
- Doesn't use very much memory as all the sorting is done using the original list.

Use a bubble sort to order this list (greatest first):

Newcastle, Liverpool, Blackpool, Chelsea, Barcelona, Stevenage Reserves, Sunderland

Cons
- It's an inefficient way to sort a list — for a list of n items, the worst case scenario would involve you doing $\frac{n(n-1)}{2}$ comparisons.
- Due to being inefficient, the bubble sort algorithm is pretty slow for very large lists of items.

But Miss, the teams are already sorted.

My friend's always happy, you know the type, the bubbly sort...

When following an algorithm there are no shortcuts, just follow the instructions from start to finish. A common mistake is to forget the final pass because you realise that the list is already in order, remember that you should always show a pass when nothing changes to complete the algorithm as a computer would.

Sorting Algorithms

The other sorting algorithm you'll need to learn is the merge sort — it splits a list apart and then magically merges it back together in the correct order. I really hope you're ready to see something special.

A Merge Sort Splits the list apart then Merges it back together

The merge sort algorithm is an example of a <u>divide-and-conquer</u> algorithm and takes advantage of two facts:

- Small lists are <u>easier to sort</u> than large lists.
- It's easier to merge <u>two ordered lists</u> than two unordered lists.

MERGE SORT ALGORITHM	1) <u>Split</u> the list in <u>half</u> (the smaller lists are called <u>sub-lists</u>) — the second sub-list should start at the <u>middle item</u> (see p4). 2) Keep repeating step 1) on each sub-list until <u>all the lists</u> only contain <u>one item</u>. 3) <u>Merge pairs</u> of sub-lists so that each sub-list has twice as many items. Each time you merge sub-lists, <u>sort the items</u> into the right order. 4) Repeat step 3) until you've merged <u>all the sub-lists</u> together.

EXAMPLE: Use the merge sort algorithm to write these letters in alphabetical order.

1) <u>Split</u> the original list of 8 items into <u>two lists</u>, the second list should start at the $(8 + 1) \div 2 = 4.5 = $ <u>5th item</u>.

2) Carry on <u>splitting</u> the sub-lists until each list only has <u>one item</u> in it.

3) <u>Merge</u> and <u>order</u> sub-lists back together. Note that merging is always performed on <u>two ordered lists</u> and is <u>very simple</u> to do. E.g.

> Compare <u>F</u> and <u>A</u> — <u>move A</u> to the new list.
> Compare <u>F</u> and <u>L</u> — <u>move F</u> to the new list.
> Compare <u>P</u> and <u>L</u> — <u>move L</u> to the new list.
> <u>P</u> is the <u>last item</u> in the new list.

4) Keep <u>merging</u> sub-lists until you only have <u>one list</u>.

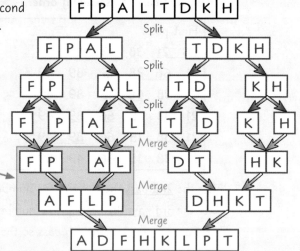

You'll often be unable to <u>split</u> or <u>merge</u> lists <u>evenly</u>. For example, sometimes you'll have to merge a list containing <u>two items</u> with a list containing <u>one item</u> to make a list of <u>three items</u>.

Pros	Cons
• In general, it's much <u>more efficient</u> and <u>quicker</u> than the bubble sort algorithm (p5) for <u>large lists</u>, and has a <u>similar running time</u> for <u>short lists</u>. • It has a very <u>consistent running time</u> regardless of how ordered the items in the original list are.	• Even if the list is <u>already sorted</u>, it still goes through the whole <u>splitting</u> and <u>merging</u> process, so a bubble sort may be <u>quicker</u> in some cases. • It uses <u>more memory</u> than the bubble sort because it has to create additional lists.

Due to its efficiency, the merge sort algorithm (or variations of it) are used in many programming languages such as Java™, Python and Perl as the primary sorting algorithm.

Merging a visit to my grandma's with a paintball trip went badly...

When doing a merge sort it's important process — if you only show the merging I think the key thing that we can all take that you show the splitting process <u>and</u> the merging process then you've only shown half the algorithm. from this page is to never merge-sort your pets.

Revision Questions for Section One

Well that's <u>algorithms</u> all <u>done</u> and <u>dusted</u>. Or so you thought — just wait until you start <u>Section Two</u>.
- Try these questions and <u>tick off each one</u> when you <u>get it right</u>.
- When you've done <u>all the questions</u> for a topic and are <u>completely happy</u> with it, tick off the topic.

Computational Thinking (p1) ☑

1) What is meant by: a) decomposition?   b) abstraction?
2) Why is using algorithmic thinking useful when solving a problem?
3) Outline the decomposition, abstraction and algorithmic processes for choosing a film at the cinema.

Pseudo-code and Flowcharts (p2-3) ☑

4) What is pseudo-code? Give three features of well-written pseudo-code.
5) What are the benefits of writing algorithms in pseudo-code rather than a programming language?
6) Draw the five box types used on flowcharts and say what each one is used for.
7) What do sequences, selections and iterations look like on a flowchart?
8)* Draw a flowchart to check if a new username is valid. Usernames should be at least
    5 characters long and unique. If it's invalid, the algorithm should give the reason why
    and get the user to enter another username.

Search Algorithms (p4) ☑

9) What are the four steps of the binary search algorithm?
10) What are the four steps of a linear search algorithm?
11)* Here's a fascinating list of British towns and cities:

    Ashington, Brecon, Chester, Dagenham, Morpeth, Usk, Watford

    a) Use a binary search to find "Morpeth" in this list:
    b) Now do the same using a linear search.
12) What are the benefits and drawbacks of using a linear search over a binary search?

Sorting Algorithms (p5-6) ☐

13) a)   What are the five steps of the bubble sort algorithm?
    b)* Use the bubble sort algorithm to sort these fruit into alphabetical order:
        Orange,   Banana,   Apple,   Peach,   Grape,   Lime
14) What are the four steps of the merge sort algorithm?
15)*Here is a list of numbers:

    8, 7, 5, 1, 3, 6, 4, 2

    a) Use the merge sort algorithm to sort this list into ascending order.
    b) Use the bubble sort algorithm to sort this list into descending order.
16) Outline the strengths and weaknesses of the following sorting algorithms:
    a) bubble sort   b)   merge sort
17) Perform a beauty sort on my pets.

*Answers on p73

Programming Basics — Data Types

Ah my favourite section of the book — it's time to get to grips with some programming...

Everything we cover in this section will work slightly differently in different programming languages, but the principles are the same and that's what you need to learn for the exam.

In this section, examples of code will be given in these boxes and will be written in pseudo-code (p2).

The output of the code will be shown in this box.

Programming languages have Five Main Data Types

1) Programming languages store data as different <u>types</u>. You need to learn the ones in this table...

Data type	Pseudo-code	Characteristics	Examples
Integer	INT	Whole numbers only.	0, 6, 10293, −999
Real (or float)	REAL	Numbers that have a decimal part.	0.15, −5.87, 100.0
Boolean	BOOL	Can only take one of two values, usually TRUE or FALSE.	True/False, 1/0, yes/no
Character	CHAR	A single letter, number, symbol.	'A', 'k', '5', '–', '$'
String	STRING	Used to represent text, it is a collection of characters.	'FsTmQ2', '$money$'

2) Each data type is allocated a different amount of <u>memory</u>.

3) Using the correct data types makes code more <u>memory efficient</u>, <u>robust</u> (hard to break) and <u>predictable</u>.

Data type	Typical amount of memory taken up
Integer	2 bytes or 4 bytes.
Real	4 bytes or 8 bytes.
Boolean	1 bit is needed but 1 byte is usually used.
Character	1 byte
String	1 byte for every character in the string.

Programming languages can be <u>weakly typed</u> or <u>strongly typed</u>. Weakly typed languages will try to <u>convert</u> data types to <u>avoid errors</u>, however this can lead to <u>unpredictable results</u>. Strongly typed languages won't try to convert data types and so will produce <u>more errors</u> but more <u>predictable results</u>.

You can Change from one Data Type to another

1) Languages have <u>functions</u> (p22) that let you manually convert between data types — this is known as <u>casting</u>. Different languages will do this in <u>different ways</u> but the principle is the same:

STRING_TO_INT('1')   Converts the <u>string '1'</u> to the <u>integer 1</u>.

STRING_TO_REAL('1.0')   Converts the <u>string '1.0'</u> to the <u>real 1.0</u>

INT_TO_STRING(1)   Converts the <u>integer 1</u> to the <u>string '1'</u>.

REAL_TO_STRING(1.0)   Converts the <u>real 1.0</u> to the <u>string '1.0'</u>

2) It's important to realise that the <u>integer 1</u>, the <u>real 1.0</u> and the <u>strings '1'</u> and <u>'1.0'</u> are all different.

3) You can also find the <u>ASCII code</u> (see p39) of <u>characters</u> and vice versa using these functions.

CHAR_TO_CODE('b')   Converts the <u>character 'b'</u> into its <u>ASCII code 98</u>.

CODE_TO_CHAR(98)   Converts the <u>ASCII code 98</u> into its equivalent <u>character 'b'</u>.

Using the Correct Data Type for different Variables

You should be able to choose the best data type to use in different situations.

 **EXAMPLE:**   Give the appropriate data type for each of the categories in this registration form.

Initial of first name:	N
Surname:	Chapman
Age (in whole years):	27
Height (in metres):	1.64
Male or Female:	Female

Initial of first name should be stored as a character.

Surname should be stored as a string.

Age (in whole years) should be stored as an integer.

Height (in metres) should be stored as a real data type.

Male or Female could be stored as Boolean.

Will you data? Nah, she's not really my type...

Using the correct data types is a fundamental part of programming — sometimes a piece of data could take different data types and you'll have to decide which is best based on the context of the question.

Programming Basics — Operators

Operators are <u>special characters</u> that perform certain functions. You'll already be used to using operators in maths, but it's important to know how they work in computer science too.

The Basic Arithmetic Operators are straightforward

1) The arithmetic operators take <u>two values</u> and perform a maths <u>function</u> on them.

2) <u>Addition</u>, <u>subtraction</u>, <u>multiplication</u> and <u>division</u> operators do what you'd expect.

3) The <u>DIV operator</u> returns the <u>whole number part</u> of a division and the <u>MOD operator</u> gives the <u>remainder</u>.

Dividing integers might behave oddly in some programming languages, e.g. 5 / 2 may give the answer 2 instead of 2.5...

...using DIV and MOD can avoid these issues.

Function	Typical Operator	Example	Result
Addition	+	5 + 5	10
Subtraction	–	3 – 10	–7
Multiplication	*	4 * 8	32
Division	/	7.5 / 5	1.5
Integer division (quotient)	DIV	20 DIV 3	6
Remainder (modulus)	MOD or %	20 MOD 3	2

4) The first four operators in the table above work on <u>integers</u> and <u>real</u> data values (or combinations of the two). DIV and MOD are for <u>integers only</u>.

5) Computers follow the rule of <u>BODMAS</u> (Brackets, Other, Division, Multiplication, Addition & Subtraction) — so <u>take care</u> when using operators to make sure your code is actually doing what you want it to. E.g. 2 + 8 * 2 will give 18. To do the addition first, use brackets: (2 + 8) * 2 will give 20.

Assignment and Comparison Operators

The <u>assignment operator</u>, ← (or =), is used to <u>assign values</u> to <u>constants</u> or <u>variables</u> (see next pg).

The name of the constant or variable should be on the <u>left hand side</u> of the ←.

```
total ← 25
cost ← total * 3
n ← n + 5
```

Whatever you're assigning to it should be on the <u>right hand side</u>.

This increases the value of n by 5.

<u>Comparison operators</u> compare the expression on their <u>left hand side</u> to the expression on their <u>right hand side</u> and produce a <u>Boolean value</u> (either true or false).

Comparison operator	What it means	Evaluates to True	Evaluates to False
= (or ==)	Is equal to	5 = 5	5 = 8
≠ (or <> or !=)	Is not equal to	6 ≠ 7	6 ≠ 6
<	Is less than	4 < 10	3 < 2
>	Is greater than	15 > 9	10 > 12
≤ (or <=)	Is less than or equal to	7 ≤ 8	11 ≤ 10
≥ (or >=)	Is greater than or equal to	3 ≥ 3	9 ≥ 12

1) Many programming languages use "=" for the <u>assignment operator</u> and "==" for the <u>comparison operator</u>. A common mistake is to get them the wrong way round — you'll know if you've used them <u>incorrectly</u> because your code won't do what you were expecting.

2) In this book we'll always use ← for assignment and = for "is equal to" so that it is clear when values are being assigned and when we are doing a comparison.

All these operators and not a surgeon in sight, PANIC...

Operators are fundamental to programming, so make sure you get to grips with them now. In your exam they'll use the operators on this page but the programming language you study might be a bit different.

Constants and Variables

Now that you know about the different data types and operations it's time to look at constants and variables.
As you can probably tell by the names, constants remain the same and variables can be changed.

Data Values can be Constants or Variables

1) Data values can be stored as constants or variables.

2) The name of the constant or variable is linked to a memory location that stores the data value.
The size of the memory location depends on the data type (see p8).

3) A constant is assigned a value at design time that can't be changed. If you attempt to change
the value of a constant in a program then the interpreter or compiler (see p29) will return an error.

4) Variables on the other hand can change value which makes them far more useful than constants.

5) In many programming languages, constants and variables need to be declared before you can use them.
When writing pseudo-code they're often just declared when you want to assign a value to them.
This can be done in different ways:

Here are two ways of declaring PRESSURE as a
constant and assigning it the value of 30. Upper
case letters are often used when naming constants.

```
constant PRESSURE as INT ← 30
constant PRESSURE ← 30
```

← The first example in
each case specifies
the data type as well.

Here are three ways of declaring temperature as a
variable and assigning it the value of 20.5. The var
keyword can be used to make it clear that it's a variable.

```
var temperature as REAL ← 20.5
var temperature ← 20.5
temperature ← 20.5
```

To make code easier to follow, programmers usually give variables and constants descriptive names.
They will also follow standard naming conventions when naming variables. For example, by
capitalising the first letter of each word (apart from the first), like tempInOven or pressureInPot.

Identifying Constants and Variables in Programs

EXAMPLE: In a multi-event athletics competition, athletes get 5 points for winning
an event and 2 points for coming second. Otherwise they get 0 points.
This program calculates the total number of points that an athlete has.

```
firsts ← USERINPUT
seconds ← USERINPUT
OUTPUT (5 * firsts + 2 * seconds)
```

a) Rewrite the program so that all the variables are declared with data types and initial values.

The two variables are
firsts and seconds. They
should both be declared
as integers as there are a
whole number of events.

```
var firsts as INT ← 0
var seconds as INT ← 0
firsts ← USERINPUT
seconds ← USERINPUT
OUTPUT (5 * firsts + 2 * seconds)
```

The initial value of each
variable is set to 0.

b) Give two reasons for assigning the values 5 and 2 to constants.

• They don't need to be changed during the running of the program.

• If the points awarded for each event was changed you'd only need
to change the value given in the declaration of the constant. ← This is an example of
improving the maintainability
(p25) of the program.

A constant, a variable... and finally a constant. Time starts now...

You can't change the data type of a variable, only the value.
But as you saw on p8 you can use a casting function to return
a different data type, which you can then assign to a new variable:

```
cost ← 50
stringCost ← INT_TO_STRING(cost)
```

This converts the integer 50 to the
string '50' and stores it in stringCost.

Strings

Remember from page 8 that strings are a data type made up of characters — these characters are
<u>alphanumeric</u> (letters, numbers, spaces, symbols, etc.). Now you'll see how you can manipulate them.

Strings are written inside Quotation Marks

In this book you'll see strings written inside <u>single
quotation marks</u> ', but in some programming languages
you might see <u>double quotation marks</u> being used ".

```
string1 ← 'Output me, I am a string.'
OUTPUT string1
```
```
Output me, I am a string.
```

Strings can be <u>joined together</u> to form
new strings — this is called <u>concatenation</u>.
It's often done using the <u>+ operator</u>.

```
string1 ← 'My favourite colour is'
string2 ← 'purple.'
newString ← string1 + ' ' + string2
OUTPUT newString
```

The + operator joins
the strings together.

A space character has
been added between
the two strings.

```
My favourite colour is purple.
```

Programs let you Manipulate Strings in a variety of ways

1) Before getting started on string manipulation you should know
    that the <u>characters</u> in a string are usually numbered <u>starting at 0</u>.

```
0 1 2 3 4 5
S P Y I N G
```

2) Here are some common <u>string manipulation</u> functions
    that you'll need to learn for your exam.

Pseudo-code function	Operation	Example
LEN(string)	Returns the number of characters in the string.	LEN('Hello') returns 5
POSITION(string, character)	Returns the position of the first occurrence of a certain character in the given string.	POSITION('Hello', 'o') returns 4 POSITION('Hello', 'l') returns 2
SUBSTRING(x, y, string)	Extracts a substring from the original string starting at position x and finishing at position y.	SUBSTRING(0, 3, 'Hello') returns 'Hell'

EXAMPLE:

An electricity company generates a customer's 7 character username from:
*   the first 3 letters of their town.
*   the customer's age when they sign up (2 digits).
*   the last letter of the customer's surname.

Write an algorithm to generate a username for any customer given that
their data is stored under the variables town, age and surname.

Start by working out how to <u>extract</u> the information from <u>each variable</u>...

1) `SUBSTRING(0, 2, town)` ← This extracts the <u>first 3 characters</u> from the customer's town.

2) `INT_TO_STRING(age)` ← <u>Converts</u> the customer's age to a <u>string</u> (p8).

3) `n ← LEN(surname)`
    `SUBSTRING(n-1, n-1, surname)` ← Finds the <u>length</u> of the <u>surname</u> so that it can take the <u>last character</u>.
    Remember, the last character is in the n–1th position.

... then combine the code into a <u>single algorithm</u> at the end.

```
n ← LEN(surname)
username ← SUBSTRING(0, 2, town) + INT_TO_STRING(age) + SUBSTRING(n-1, n-1, surname)
```

I hope you don't just think I'm stringing you along...

Any text that is input or output from a program will be a string, so it's important that you can manipulate
them like you've got them wrapped around your little finger. As well as the functions above, the examiners
might throw a more obscure one at you in the exam. Luckily they'll also show you exactly how it works.

Program Flow — Selection

The flow of a program is the order that the steps are carried out in. One way that you can control the program flow is by using selection statements — but first, here's how to get your programs to interact with the user.

Programs need to be able to Interact with a User

1) It's really handy for programs to be able to get information from and give information to the user — this is done through the input and output devices.

2) Inputs can be received from many devices, e.g. keyboard, mouse, webcam or microphone.

3) Outputs are typically displayed visually on the monitor or as sound from the speakers.

4) When writing pseudo-code we usually assume that inputs are from a keyboard and outputs will be displayed on a monitor (typically as text).

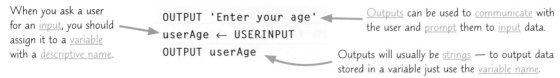

When you ask a user for an input, you should assign it to a variable with a descriptive name.

```
OUTPUT 'Enter your age'
userAge ← USERINPUT
OUTPUT userAge
```

Outputs can be used to communicate with the user and prompt them to input data.

Outputs will usually be strings — to output data stored in a variable just use the variable name.

IF statements usually have an IF-THEN-ELSE structure

1) IF statements allow you to check if a condition is true or false, and carry out different actions depending on the outcome. You can think about them as a flowchart.

2) Here is a program that can verify if the user knows a certain passcode before granting access.

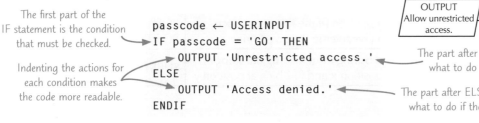

The first part of the IF statement is the condition that must be checked.

Indenting the actions for each condition makes the code more readable.

```
passcode ← USERINPUT
IF passcode = 'GO' THEN
    OUTPUT 'Unrestricted access.'
ELSE
    OUTPUT 'Access denied.'
ENDIF
```

The part after THEN tells the program what to do if the condition is true.

The part after ELSE tells the program what to do if the condition is false.

3) If there is nothing for the program to do when the condition is false, leave out the 'else' part.

Nested IF statements allow multiple outputs

1) More complex IF statements can be made by putting one IF statement inside another one — this type of selection statement is called a nested IF statement.

2) Nested IF statements allow you to check more conditions once you've established that the previous condition is true or false.

If the first condition is true, it will check the second condition...

If the first condition is false, it will run this else statement — all access is denied.

Indentation lets the reader see where each IF statement begins and ends.

```
userType ← USERINPUT
passcode ← USERINPUT
IF passcode = 'GO' THEN
    IF userType = 'Teacher' THEN
        OUTPUT 'Unrestricted access.'
    ELSE
        OUTPUT 'Restricted access.'
    ENDIF
ELSE
    OUTPUT 'Access denied.'
ENDIF
```

If the second condition is true then unrestricted access is allowed.

If the second condition is false then restricted access is allowed.

IF you understand IF statements THEN make yourself a brew...

IF statements are used all the time when writing code — they really are a programmer's best friend. Whenever there is a decision to be made, a friendly IF statement will always be there to help you out.

Program Flow — Selection

A couple more selection statements coming right up, starting with an ELSE-IF statement. Careful with these ones — they might look similar to nested IF statements, but they are different. Have a look below...

ELSE-IF statements check conditions until one is True

1) <u>ELSE-IF statements</u> are used to check <u>multiple conditions</u> and give <u>different outputs</u> depending on which condition is <u>true</u>.

2) They are different from nested IF statements as they only <u>check more conditions</u> if the <u>previous condition</u> is <u>false</u> — e.g. IF the <u>first condition</u> is <u>true</u> then they <u>won't check</u> the others.

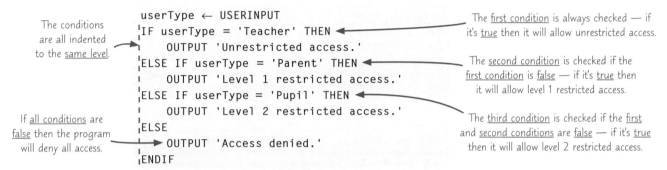

The conditions are all indented to the <u>same level</u>.

```
userType ← USERINPUT
IF userType = 'Teacher' THEN
    OUTPUT 'Unrestricted access.'
ELSE IF userType = 'Parent' THEN
    OUTPUT 'Level 1 restricted access.'
ELSE IF userType = 'Pupil' THEN
    OUTPUT 'Level 2 restricted access.'
ELSE
    OUTPUT 'Access denied.'
ENDIF
```

The <u>first condition</u> is always checked — if it's <u>true</u> then it will allow unrestricted access.

The <u>second condition</u> is checked if the <u>first condition</u> is <u>false</u> — if it's <u>true</u> then it will allow level 1 restricted access.

The <u>third condition</u> is checked if the <u>first</u> and <u>second conditions</u> are <u>false</u> — if it's <u>true</u> then it will allow level 2 restricted access.

If <u>all conditions</u> are <u>false</u> then the program will deny all access.

CASE Statements check the value of a Variable

1) Instead of checking to see if a condition is true or false, <u>CASE statements</u> (sometimes called **SWITCH** statements) can check if a <u>variable</u> has <u>specific values</u>.

2) They're used when you want a program to perform <u>different actions</u> for <u>different values</u> of the <u>same variable</u>.

3) Here is a program that can be used to <u>count votes</u> in an election.

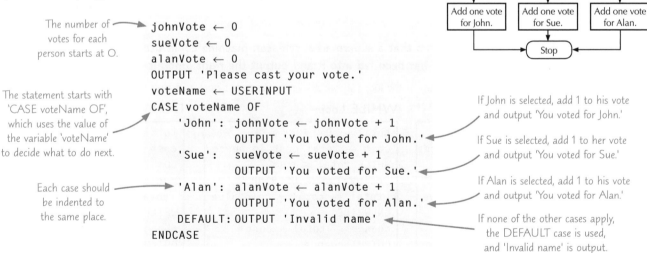

The number of votes for each person starts at 0.

The statement starts with 'CASE voteName OF', which uses the value of the variable 'voteName' to decide what to do next.

Each case should be indented to the same place.

```
johnVote ← 0
sueVote ← 0
alanVote ← 0
OUTPUT 'Please cast your vote.'
voteName ← USERINPUT
CASE voteName OF
    'John': johnVote ← johnVote + 1
            OUTPUT 'You voted for John.'
    'Sue':  sueVote ← sueVote + 1
            OUTPUT 'You voted for Sue.'
    'Alan': alanVote ← alanVote + 1
            OUTPUT 'You voted for Alan.'
    DEFAULT: OUTPUT 'Invalid name'
ENDCASE
```

If John is selected, add 1 to his vote and output 'You voted for John.'

If Sue is selected, add 1 to her vote and output 'You voted for Sue.'

If Alan is selected, add 1 to his vote and output 'You voted for Alan.'

If none of the other cases apply, the DEFAULT case is used, and 'Invalid name' is output.

4) CASE statements have a <u>similar structure</u> to ELSE-IF statements but they give a <u>neater</u> way to test <u>different values</u> of a variable — this makes them easier than ELSE-IF statements to <u>maintain</u>.

5) The <u>drawback</u> of CASE statements is that they can <u>only check</u> the value of <u>one variable</u>. ELSE-IF statements can check if <u>multiple conditions</u> are true.

> ELSE-IF and CASE statements can also be used to make more complex <u>nested selection</u> statements just like the nested IF statements on p12.

Can't decide what to have for lunch? Use a selection statement...

CASE statements don't have to include a DEFAULT case, just like how IF statements don't need an ELSE. In some cases (like the example above) putting one in can help to make your program more robust.

Program Flow — Iteration

Now it's time to have a look at some <u>iteration statements</u>. The statements on this page are all <u>indefinite</u> iteration statements — so the number of times that they repeat depends on a <u>condition</u>.

All these Loops are controlled by Conditions

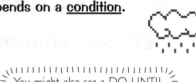

You might also see a DO-UNTIL loop — this does the same thing as a REPEAT-UNTIL loop.

<u>REPEAT-UNTIL</u>, <u>WHILE</u> and <u>DO-WHILE</u> loops are easy to get mixed up — they're very similar but with subtle differences that you need to know:

REPEAT-UNTIL LOOPS
- Controlled by a condition at the <u>end of the loop</u>.
- Keep going <u>until</u> the condition is <u>true</u> (i.e. while it is false).
- <u>Always run</u> the code inside them <u>at least once</u>.
- You get an <u>infinite loop</u> if the condition is <u>never true</u>.

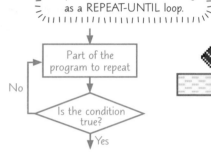
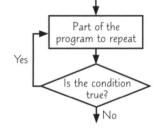

WHILE LOOPS
- Controlled by a condition at the <u>start of the loop</u>.
- Keep going <u>while</u> the condition is <u>true</u> (i.e. until it is false).
- <u>Never run</u> the code inside them if the condition is initially <u>false</u>.
- You get an <u>infinite loop</u> if the condition is <u>always true</u>.

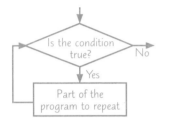

DO-WHILE LOOPS
- Controlled by a condition at the <u>end of the loop</u>.
- Keep going <u>while</u> the condition is <u>true</u> (i.e. until it is false).
- <u>Always run</u> the code inside them <u>at least once</u>.
- You get an <u>infinite loop</u> if the condition is <u>always true</u>.

EXAMPLE: Write an algorithm that a supermarket self-scan machine could use to check if enough money has been fed into it and output the right amount of change.

You could write an algorithm using any of the loops shown above — the code before and after the loop is exactly the same.

REPEAT-UNTIL Loop:

```
total ← 0
cost ← total cost in pence
REPEAT
  coinValue ← USERINPUT
  total ← total + coinValue
UNTIL total ≥ cost
change ← total - cost
OUTPUT change
```

The loop starts at <u>REPEAT</u> and ends when the <u>UNTIL</u> condition is <u>true</u> — when the total is greater than or equal to the cost.

WHILE Loop:

```
total ← 0
cost ← total cost in pence
WHILE total < cost
  coinValue ← USERINPUT
  total ← total + coinValue
ENDWHILE
change ← total - cost
OUTPUT change
```

The loop starts by checking the <u>WHILE</u> condition is <u>true</u> and keeps repeating until it is <u>false</u> — when the total is greater than or equal to the cost.

DO-WHILE Loop:

```
total ← 0
cost ← total cost in pence
DO
  coinValue ← USERINPUT
  total ← total + coinValue
WHILE total < cost
change ← total - cost
OUTPUT change
```

The loop starts at <u>DO</u> and repeats until the <u>WHILE</u> condition is <u>false</u> — when the total is greater than or equal to the cost.

All of these loops work exactly the same when cost > 0. If the cost is 0, the WHILE loop won't expect an input, whereas the REPEAT-UNTIL and DO-WHILE loops will.

All these loops and not a roller coaster in sight, what a shame...

It's important that you learn the similarities and differences between all of these condition-controlled loops so that they don't all merge into one. The key thing is recognising exactly when the loop will stop.

Program Flow — Iteration

The final type of iteration statement you need to know about is the FOR loop — it's a type of <u>definite</u> iteration so it will repeat for the exact number of times you tell it to. What a well-behaved little iteration statement.

FOR Loops are an example of a Count-Controlled Loop

1) <u>FOR loops</u> will repeat the code inside them a fixed number of times. The number of times that the code repeats will depend on an <u>initial value</u>, <u>end value</u> and sometimes a <u>step count</u>.

2) For example, for k ← 1 TO 10 STEP 3 will count up from 1 to 10 in steps of 3, so k ← 1, k ← 4, k ← 7 and k ← 10. If no step count is given the count will increase by 1 each time.

The FOR loop repeats the code between FOR and ENDFOR.

3) The <u>number of times</u> the loop repeats can also be set as the <u>program runs</u> — e.g. FOR k ← 1 TO x, where x is a variable.

4) FOR loops can also use the count <u>within the loop</u> — in the example on the right, k is used to keep track of how many votes have been cast.

Loops can contain other types of statement — the CASE statement used here is from p13.

```
johnVote ← 0
sueVote ← 0
alanVote ← 0
FOR k ← 1 TO 100          ← Allows 100 votes to be cast.
    OUTPUT 'Please cast your vote.'
    voteName ← USERINPUT
    CASE voteName OF
        'John': johnVote ← johnVote + 1
                OUTPUT 'You voted for John.'
        'Sue':  sueVote ← sueVote + 1
                OUTPUT 'You've voted for Sue.'
        'Alan': alanVote ← alanVote + 1
                OUTPUT 'You voted for Alan.'
    ENDCASE
    OUTPUT INT_TO_STRING(k) + ' total votes'
ENDFOR
```

The value of k can be used anywhere within the loop.

Nested Iteration statements have Loops Within loops

1) Nested iteration statements will typically just have <u>one loop</u> inside <u>another loop</u> (an <u>outer</u> loop and an <u>inner</u> loop). But they can get quite complicated when you start <u>adding more loops</u> — you get loops within loops within loops... etc.

2) <u>Every time</u> the outer loop repeats, the inner loop completes a <u>full set</u> of iterations.

3) The example below shows a <u>FOR loop</u> inside a <u>REPEAT-UNTIL loop</u>. The algorithm is for a darts practice machine, where the player tries to get a score of <u>100 or more</u> in <u>3 darts</u>, and the machine counts <u>how many attempts</u> it takes them to do it.

Nested iteration is really useful when you're working with two-dimensional arrays — see p19.

At the start of each iteration of the REPEAT loop, the number of attempts taken increases by 1 and the current total is reset to 0.

The REPEAT loop ends when the player scores 100 points or more in one round.

```
attempt ← 0
REPEAT
    attempt ← attempt + 1
    total ← 0
    FOR dart ← 1 TO 3
        OUTPUT 'Enter score for throw'
        score ← USERINPUT
        total ← total + score
    ENDFOR
UNTIL total ≥ 100
OUTPUT INT_TO_STRING(attempt) + ' attempts taken.'
```

Each time you go through the REPEAT loop, the FOR loop repeats 3 times.

On every iteration of the FOR loop, the player enters their score and it is added to their total for that attempt.

FOR k ← 0 TO 1 000 000, send us a batch of muffins, ENDFOR...

When you're putting nested iteration statements into your own programs, you can use any combination of definite and indefinite loops. Just be careful that you don't get stuck looping around forever and ever.

Boolean Operators

Boolean operators work with Boolean values to produce a Boolean answer — that's a whole lot of Booleans in one sentence. Learn the stuff on this page and one day you'll be a Booleanaire, just like me.

AND, OR and NOT are the only Boolean Operators you'll need

1) It doesn't make sense to use the arithmetic operators on things that are either true or false so instead you use the Boolean operators <u>AND</u>, <u>OR</u> and <u>NOT</u>.

Boolean operator	Examples that return true	Examples that return false
AND	$3 < 5$ AND $2 > 1$	$4 \leq 5$ AND $10 > 20$
OR	$1 > 8$ OR $2 = 2$	$1 = 8$ OR $2 < 2$
NOT	NOT$(5 > 8)$	NOT$(10 > 6)$

> In some code you might see AND written as &&, OR written as || and NOT written as !

2) Just like with numerical operators, you can <u>combine Boolean operators</u> — it's important that you use <u>brackets</u> in long Boolean expressions to let the computer know which part to do <u>first</u>. <u>Boolean operations</u> are carried out in the following <u>order</u>: brackets, NOT, AND then OR.

Boolean Operators can be used in Conditions

Boolean operators can be used in selection and iteration statements (p12-15) to check <u>multiple conditions</u>.

1. Karen and Stu are playing a 'best out of 10' game. The game should end when one of them wins 6 rounds or they both win 5 rounds. Write an algorithm to keep score in the game.

```
karenRounds ← 0
stuRounds ← 0
REPEAT
    OUTPUT 'Enter the name of the round winner'
    roundWinner ← USERINPUT
    CASE roundWinner OF ←
        'Karen': karenRounds ← karenRounds + 1
        'Stu': stuRounds ← stuRounds + 1
    ENDCASE
UNTIL karenRounds = 6 OR stuRounds = 6 OR (karenRounds = 5 AND stuRounds = 5)
```

There's a CASE statement within the loop. This is where good indentation in your pseudo-code is key.

The REPEAT-UNTIL loop stops when one of these three conditions is met.

2. In a computer game a character's status depends on three variables: hunger, hydration and comfort. If any of the conditions on the right are met then the character dies, otherwise they are alive.

- Any of the variables are equal to 0.
- Any two of the variables are less than 20.
- All three of the variables are less than 40.

Write an algorithm to work out the status of the character.

```
IF hunger = 0 OR hydration = 0 OR comfort = 0 THEN
    alive ← false
ELSE IF (hunger < 20 AND hydration < 20) OR (hunger < 20 AND comfort < 20)
        OR (hydration < 20 AND comfort < 20) THEN
    alive ← false
ELSE IF hunger < 40 AND hydration < 40 AND comfort < 40 THEN
    alive ← false
ELSE
    alive ← true
ENDIF
```

Anyone caught Boolean other pupils will be given detention...

Make sure you can use Boolean operators in your programs — they can save lots of work by letting you check lots of conditions at the same time. There is more about how Boolean operators work on p31-32.

Random Number Generation

Random numbers are really useful when you don't want your programs to do the same thing every time. They can be used to simulate random real-life events, e.g. rolling a dice, picking raffle tickets, etc.

Random Numbers are useful when making Games

1) Random numbers can be used in <u>simple games</u> when the programmer wants a number to be <u>unknown</u> — even the programmer themselves won't know what it's going to be.

2) Most programming languages have functions to <u>generate random numbers</u> — in pseudo-code, <u>random integers</u> can be generated using this function:

RANDOM_INT(x, y)

Generates a random integer between x and y (including x and y).

3) Here is an example of how random numbers can be used to simulate a roll of a <u>6-sided dice</u>.

Will randomly generate either 1, 2, 3, 4, 5 or 6 and assign it to the variable 'roll'.

```
roll ← RANDOM_INT(1, 6)
OUTPUT roll
```

Here, the number it has randomly generated is 2.

```
2
```

4) <u>FOR loops</u> can be used when you want to generate a <u>whole bunch</u> of random numbers.

This FOR loop will generate five random numbers from 1 to 10.

```
FOR i ← 1 TO 5
    roll ← RANDOM_INT(1, 10)
    OUTPUT roll
ENDFOR
```

The output will look something like...

```
4
9
4
2
10
```

Note that the same number can be randomly generated more than once.

You can use Random Numbers to make Random Selections

1) Instead of outputting the random number that you generated, you can use it to randomly generate <u>another event</u>.

2) Suppose you want to <u>simulate a coin toss</u> — there are two outcomes, <u>heads</u> or <u>tails</u> — we can simplify this in programming terms to 0 and 1 (where 0 = heads, 1 = tails).

Heads I win, tails you lose...

```
number ← RANDOM_INT(0, 1)
IF number = 0 THEN
    OUTPUT 'Heads'
ELSE IF number = 1 THEN
    OUTPUT 'Tails'
ENDIF
```

Randomly generates either 0 or 1.

Technically, you could have an ELSE statement at the bottom without the condition, because there are only two possible outcomes.

3) Random numbers are really handy to use with <u>arrays</u> (see p18-19). You can generate a <u>random number</u> then pick the element in that <u>position</u> of the array.

Uses the random number to select a piece of fruit from the array.

```
fruits ← ['Mango', 'Banana', 'Pear', 'Peach']
number ← RANDOM_INT(0, 3)
chosenFruit ← fruits[number]
OUTPUT number
OUTPUT 'Today you should eat a ' + chosenFruit
```

Randomly generates either 0, 1, 2 or 3.

The random number generated was 3, so the fruit that was chosen was 'Peach' — as numbering in an array starts at 0.

```
3
Today you should eat a Peach
```

1, 1, 1, 1, 1, 1, 1 — I think my random number generator is broken...

The random numbers that are generated in a programming language are called pseudo-random numbers because they aren't completely random, they just look like they are. They are usually generated by following a complex algorithm which means that they will have a pattern — it's just very hard to see it...

Arrays

When you need to store data within a program you can do it using variables. But if you have lots of similar data to store, then using variables for each one is inefficient and that's where arrays come in. Hip, hip, array!

Arrays are used to store multiple Data Values

1) An array is a data structure that can store a group of data values, of the same type, under one name.

2) Each piece of data in an array is called an element — each element can be accessed using its position (or index) in the array.

A data structure is a format for storing data — other data structures include records and files.

3) Arrays are most helpful when you have lots of related data that you want to store and it doesn't make sense to use separate variables — e.g. the names of pupils in a class, marks in a test, etc.

4) Just like variables, some languages require you to declare arrays before you use them.

One-Dimensional Arrays are like Lists

The easiest way to get your head around one-dimensional arrays is to picture them as lists. Different languages have lots of fancy ways to create and update arrays. Here are the ones you'll need to learn for your exam:

Topics I Love
Networks
Logic
Algorithms
Programming

1) Creating arrays — just like variables, you start off with the array name and the assignment operator. Then put your data values inside square brackets [ ] with commas separating each value.

    rowers ← ['Mark', 'Adam', 'Shelly', 'Tobias']

    Here the strings 'Mark', 'Adam', 'Shelly' and 'Tobias' are in positions 0, 1, 2 and 3 of the rowers array.

2) Retrieving elements from an array can be done by using the name of the array and the element's position. Remember that positions are numbered starting at 0.

    OUTPUT rowers[0]

    Mark

3) Changing elements is done by reassigning the array position to a different data value.

    Replaces the rower in position 0 with 'Tamal'.

    rowers[0] ← 'Tamal'
    OUTPUT rowers

    ['Tamal', 'Adam', 'Shelly', 'Tobias']

    Notice that 'Mark' has been completely removed from the array.

4) The number of elements in an array can be found using the LEN() function — just like for strings (see p11).

    LEN(rowers)

    4

Combining these array functions with **FOR loops** (see p15) will give you a systematic way of accessing and changing all of the elements in an array. Amongst other things, FOR loops can be used to search for specific elements, or make a similar change to lots of elements.

EXAMPLE: The numbers below are stored in an array called scores. Write an algorithm that will add 3 to each element of the scores array.

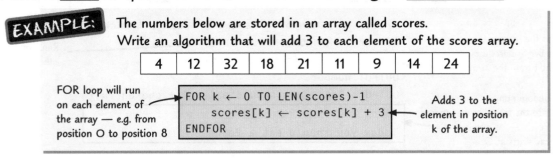

| 4 | 12 | 32 | 18 | 21 | 11 | 9 | 14 | 24 |

FOR loop will run on each element of the array — e.g. from position 0 to position 8

```
FOR k ← 0 TO LEN(scores)-1
    scores[k] ← scores[k] + 3
ENDFOR
```

Adds 3 to the element in position k of the array.

Oh, you were expecting me to make some sort of arraysing pun...

In some programming languages (e.g. C, C++, Java™) you'll find that arrays can only store one data type and that you can't change the size of them once they've been declared. In others (e.g. PHP) arrays are much more flexible data structures — they can store different data types and their size can be altered.

Arrays

Now that you've covered one-dimensional arrays, the only way is up — that's right, two-dimensional arrays. Arrays can have even more dimensions, but luckily the examiners have decided that two is enough.

Two-Dimensional Arrays are like a List Of Lists

You can think of two-dimensional arrays as <u>one-dimensional arrays</u> where <u>each element</u> is also a <u>one-dimensional array</u>.

```
trees ← [['oak', 'ash'], ['beech', 'cedar'], ['pine', 'elm']]
```

You can visualise arrays as tables or grids.

	0	1
0	oak	ash
1	beech	cedar
2	pine	elm

The <u>position</u> of an element is usually written as [a][b] or [a, b], where <u>a</u> represents the position of the one-dimensional list that the element is in and <u>b</u> represents its position within that one-dimensional list.

```
OUTPUT 'My favourite tree is ' + trees[0][0]
OUTPUT 'My 2nd favourite tree is ' + trees[2][1]
```
```
My favourite tree is oak
My 2nd favourite tree is elm
```

You can <u>change elements</u> in exactly the same way as you saw for <u>one-dimensional arrays</u> (p18).

You can also use the <u>LEN()</u> function on an <u>array</u> or on an <u>element</u> in the array.

```
LEN(trees)
```
```
3
```
```
LEN(trees[1])
```
```
2
```

Two-Dimensional Array Example

EXAMPLE: The 'scores' array has been used to store four test scores for five pupils, as shown. E.g. scores[2][0] will return the test 2 score for pupil 0, which is 5.

		Pupils				
		0	1	2	3	4
Tests	**0**	15	5	13	12	7
	1	2	14	11	14	9
	2	5	4	12	7	13
	3	6	8	18	19	15

a) Evaluate scores[3][2] / scores[1][0].

scores[3][2] = 18 and scores[1][0] = 2

So scores[3][2] / scores[1][0] = 18/2 = 9

b) Write an algorithm to count the total score of any given pupil.

As there aren't very many scores you could just add them together. E.g. for pupil 0 you could do scores[0][0] + scores[1][0] + scores[2][0] + scores[3][0]. But it's <u>better practice</u> to use a <u>loop</u> as it is easier to edit.

```
total ← 0
OUTPUT 'Enter the number of the pupil'
pupil ← USERINPUT
FOR i ← 0 TO 3
    total ← total + scores[i][pupil]
ENDFOR
OUTPUT total
```

c) The pass mark on every test was 9 or above. Write an algorithm to count the number of passes in the original array.

The passTotal variable keeps track of <u>how many values</u> are passes.

The <u>i FOR loop</u> searches each row and the <u>j FOR loop</u> searches each column.

The IF statement checks if the value in position [i][j] is a pass and <u>adds 1</u> to passTotal if it is.

Finally <u>passTotal</u> is output.

This is an example of a nested FOR loop.

```
passTotal ← 0
FOR i ← 0 TO 3
    FOR j ← 0 TO 4
        IF scores[i][j] ≥ 9 THEN
            passTotal ← passTotal + 1
        ENDIF
    ENDFOR
ENDFOR
OUTPUT INT_TO_STRING(passTotal) + ' passes.'
```

After that last pun, I'd say that I definitely deserve arrays...

Two-dimensional arrays can be used to store information about a digital image — each pixel's information can be stored as an element in the array. Programmers can then manipulate the image using array commands, e.g. changing the values of pixels, cutting rows and columns out of the image, etc.

Records

Records aren't just those big black round things that look like burnt CDs, they're also a useful data structure...

Records can contain Different Data Types

1) A <u>record</u> is a type of data structure (like an array — see p18), which means that it is used to store a collection of data values.

In the context of a database table, a record is just a row of data.

2) One of the things that makes records so useful is that, unlike arrays, they can store values with <u>different data types</u> (see p8), such as strings, integers and Booleans.

3) Each item in a record is called a <u>field</u>, and each field is given a <u>data type</u> and a <u>field name</u> when the record is created. The field name can help to <u>describe</u> the data stored in that field of the record.

Different programming languages have slight variations on record data structures. E.g. Python has dictionaries, and C has structures.

4) Records are <u>fixed in length</u>, which means that you <u>can't add extra fields</u> to them once they've been created.

Records can keep Related Information in one place

1) When you create a record structure, you can assign a <u>data type</u> and a <u>name</u> to each field:

Each field has its own data type.

```
RECORD recipes
    INT recipeNumber
    STRING recipeName
    BOOL tested
    INT score
ENDRECORD
```

The record is called 'recipes'.

'recipeNumber', 'recipeName', 'tested' and 'score' are the <u>fields</u> of the record.

2) Once you've created the structure of your record, you can <u>assign it</u> to variables:

'recipe1', 'recipe2' and 'recipe3' are all <u>variables</u> with the 'recipes' <u>record structure</u>.

```
recipe1 ← recipes(1, 'Chocolate Cake', True, 3)
recipe2 ← recipes(2, 'Lemon Slice', False, 0)
recipe3 ← recipes(3, 'Coconut Cookies', True, 8)
```

The data in each field needs to have the correct data type. E.g. the last one, 'score', should be an integer.

3) You can use the <u>variable name</u> to access a <u>whole record</u>. Or you can use the <u>variable name</u> with a <u>field name</u> to access a <u>particular item</u> of a record.

```
OUTPUT recipe1
OUTPUT recipe3.recipeName
```
```
(1, 'Chocolate Cake', True, 3)
Coconut Cookies
```

Individual items in a record can be accessed and changed.

```
recipe2.tested ← True
recipe2.score ← 6
OUTPUT recipe2.recipeName + ' scored '
       + INT_TO_STRING(recipe2.score)
```
```
Lemon Slice scored 6
```

Arrays are handy if you want to Group Records together

If you have multiple variables with the <u>same record structure</u>, you can collect them in an array.

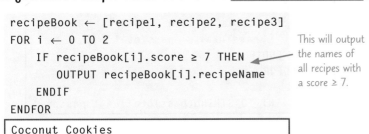

```
recipeBook ← [recipe1, recipe2, recipe3]
FOR i ← 0 TO 2
    IF recipeBook[i].score ≥ 7 THEN
        OUTPUT recipeBook[i].recipeName
    ENDIF
ENDFOR
```

This will output the names of all recipes with a score ≥ 7.

```
Coconut Cookies
```

You can visualise the recipeBook array as a table:

	recipeNumber	recipeName	tested	score
0	1	Chocolate Cake	True	3
1	2	Lemon Slice	True	6
2	3	Coconut Cookies	True	8

Well, we got through all that in record time...

Records might be presented slightly differently in your exam, but the key concepts will be the same. Make sure you understand what records and fields are, and how they can be used in programming.

File Handling

File handling is all about how a program can access data and change data stored in an external file. Accessing external files makes programs more useful (like a see-through toaster) and powerful (like my new blender).

Files allow Permanent Data Storage

1) Storing data in arrays (p18-19) and records (p20) is useful when the program is running, but all the data will be lost when the program is closed.

2) It's often useful for programs to store data permanently and then access it at a later date — this is done by writing data to an external file.

3) Programming languages typically have their own commands for handling files. Most languages will have commands to open files, close files, read text from a file and write text to a file.

Always start by Opening the External File

> This page will focus on how text is stored and accessed from ".txt" files. Other text files that are commonly used are ".csv" and ".dat".

1) Before you can do anything with a file you need to open it. This is done by using an OPEN() command and assigning it to a variable.

This will open the file so that you can read or write to it. ↘

This is the name of the file you want to open. Sometimes you'll have to give the whole file path. ↙

```
newFile ← OPEN('newFile.txt')
```

2) Once a file is opened the program will start reading or writing from the beginning. As you read from or write to the file, the program keeps its place in the file (think of it like a cursor).

> Some programming languages have separate open commands depending on whether you want to read from or write to the file.

3) When you're finished reading or writing to a file you should always close it using CLOSE(). If you forget to close it then the file can remain locked and prevent others from editing it.

Read or Write to a file after it is Opened

1) After you have opened a file you can read or write to it.

2) You can write text to a file using the WRITE() or WRITELINE() commands. If the file already contains some text then you'll need to be careful that you don't overwrite it.

The WRITE() and WRITELINE() commands take two parameters. The first is the variable storing the file and the second is the text you want to write. →

```
winners ← OPEN('victory.txt')
names ← ['Jenny', 'Carlos', 'Matty', 'Anna']
FOR i ← 0 TO 3
    textToWrite ← INT_TO_STRING(i) + ' ' + names[i]
    WRITELINE(winners, textToWrite)
ENDFOR
CLOSE(winners)
```

The text file will look like this. →

```
0 Jenny
1 Carlos
2 Matty
3 Anna
```

3) You can read text from a file using READ() or READLINE().

Reads the first line of the text file as programs always start reading from the start of the file. After this command is called, the 'cursor' will be at the beginning of the second line. →

```
winners ← OPEN('victory.txt')
firstLine ← READLINE(winners)
secondLine ← READLINE(winners)
CLOSE(winners)
```

Reads the second line of the file as that's where the program is up to. After this command is called, the 'cursor' will be at the beginning of the third line. ←

4) ENDOFFILE() is another useful command. It returns 'true' if the 'cursor' is at the end of the file. It's really handy for using as the condition to tell a loop when to terminate.

```
winners ← OPEN('victory.txt')
REPEAT
    currentLine ← READLINE(winners)
    OUTPUT currentLine
UNTIL ENDOFFILE(winners)
CLOSE(winners)
```

Learning to read and write, it's like being back at primary school...

Data is stored externally so that it's not lost when the program is closed. E.g. a computer game will save your progress externally — if it was saved internally you'd lose your progress when the game was closed.

Subroutines

Subroutines (or sub programs) can be used to save time and to simplify code. By now you'll definitely have come across them even if you don't know what they are yet — all is explained on the next two pages.

Subroutines help to avoid Repeating Code

1) Subroutines are sets of instructions stored under one name — when you want your program to do the whole set of instructions you only need to call the name of the subroutine.

2) Subroutines can be either functions or procedures — the main difference is that functions always return a value and procedures do not.

3) Subroutines are very useful when you have sets of instructions that you need to repeat in different places within a program. They give your program more structure and readability whilst cutting down on the amount of code you actually need to write.

4) High-level programming languages (see p29) have common subroutines built into them. If you want one that does something more specific you can create them yourself.

```
# The max() subroutine returns the highest value.
x ← max(12, 21, 8, 9, 19)
```

5) In most subroutines you'll encounter parameters.

> Parameters are special variables used to pass values into a subroutine. For each parameter you can specify a name, a data type and a default value.

The actual values that the parameters take when the subroutine is called are sometimes called arguments.

Subroutines can carry out a Set Of Instructions

1) Subroutines don't have to take parameters...

```
SUBROUTINE welcome()
    OUTPUT 'Hello and welcome.'
    OUTPUT 'This is a procedure.'
ENDSUBROUTINE
```

...but they sometimes will.

'name' is a parameter.

```
SUBROUTINE betterWelcome(name)
    OUTPUT 'Hello ' + name + ' and welcome.'
    OUTPUT 'This is a procedure.'
ENDSUBROUTINE
```

2) Subroutines are called by typing their name (and giving parameters if necessary).

```
welcome()
```
```
Hello and welcome.
This is a procedure.
```

```
betterWelcome('Pablo')
```
```
Hello Pablo and welcome.
This is a procedure.
```

The string 'Pablo' is passed into the betterWelcome subroutine.

3) Note that subroutines that don't return a value are called procedures.

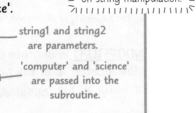

PROCEDURE SHOP
We have a strict no returns policy.

Functions will always Return a Value

1) Subroutines that return a value are called functions.

2) When a function is called it should be assigned to a variable or used in a statement otherwise the value that it returns will not be stored anywhere and will be lost.

See p11 for a reminder on string manipulation.

 **EXAMPLE:** Write a subroutine to join two strings together with a space between them and show it working on the strings 'computer' and 'science'.

Use RETURN to pass a value out of the subroutine.

The result is stored as the variable 'subject'.

```
SUBROUTINE joinStrings(string1, string2)
    RETURN string1 + ' ' + string2
ENDSUBROUTINE
subject ← joinStrings('computer', 'science')
OUTPUT subject
```
```
computer science
```

string1 and string2 are parameters.

'computer' and 'science' are passed into the subroutine.

So is a parameter longer or shorter than a kilometre?

When you're actually programming with subroutines they are written as a separate block of code to the main program. They are then used by the main program when you want to perform a specific operation.

Subroutines

Ah, just what the doctor ordered, another page on subroutines — and this one is even better. Trust me.

Subroutines can contain anything covered in this Section

EXAMPLE: Orla has been given a maths problem to add together all of the numbers between two integers (including the integers themselves) and work out if the total is divisible by 7.

Write a subroutine that Orla could use to solve the maths problem for any pair of integers.

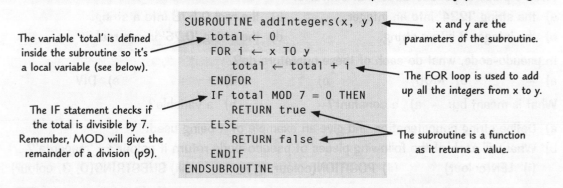

The variable 'total' is defined inside the subroutine so it's a local variable (see below).

x and y are the parameters of the subroutine.

The FOR loop is used to add up all the integers from x to y.

The IF statement checks if the total is divisible by 7. Remember, MOD will give the remainder of a division (p9).

The subroutine is a function as it returns a value.

```
SUBROUTINE addIntegers(x, y)
    total ← 0
    FOR i ← x TO y
        total ← total + i
    ENDFOR
    IF total MOD 7 = 0 THEN
        RETURN true
    ELSE
        RETURN false
    ENDIF
ENDSUBROUTINE
```

Variables can be local or global

1) All variables have a <u>scope</u> (either local or global) — the scope of a variable tells you <u>which parts</u> of the program the variable can be used in.

> *All parameters have local scope to the subroutine.*

> <u>Local variables</u> can only be used <u>within the structure</u> they're declared in — they have a <u>local scope</u>.
> <u>Global variables</u> can be used <u>any time</u> after their declaration — they have a <u>global scope</u>.

2) Variables declared inside a <u>subroutine</u> are <u>local variables</u>. They are <u>invisible</u> to the rest of the program — this means that they can't be used <u>outside</u> the subroutine.

3) The <u>advantage</u> of local variables is that their scope only extends to the subroutine they're declared in. They <u>can't affect</u> and are <u>not affected</u> by anything outside of the subroutine. It also doesn't matter if you use the <u>same variable name</u> as a local variable defined elsewhere in the program.

4) Variables in the <u>main body</u> of a program can be made into global variables using the 'GLOBAL' keyword — these variables can then be used anywhere in the program. It can be difficult to keep track of the <u>value</u> of global variables in <u>larger programs</u>.

5) The example below shows how <u>global variables</u> are used to store data outside of the subroutine.

x and y are defined <u>globally</u> — if they were declared inside the subroutine then they'd <u>reset to 0</u> each time the subroutine was called.

The subroutine is a <u>procedure</u> as it <u>doesn't</u> return a value.

The <u>parameters</u> a and b are added to the <u>global variables</u> x and y.

The program <u>keeps track</u> of the position after the first move and then applies the second move from that position.

a and b are parameters so they have <u>local scope</u> to this procedure — they're <u>invisible</u> elsewhere in the program.

```
# A subroutine to keep track of a character's x and y position.
GLOBAL x ← 0
GLOBAL y ← 0
SUBROUTINE move(a, b)
    x ← x + a
    y ← y + b
    OUTPUT '(' + INT_TO_STRING(x) + ', ' + INT_TO_STRING(y) + ')'
ENDSUBROUTINE
move(3, 5)
move(4, 7)
```

```
(3, 5)
(7, 12)
```

Sorry you can't come in, this function is for local variables only...

Subroutines are great at simplifying code and writing code in an efficient way. It's best to give variables a local scope wherever possible — that way you don't have to worry about them in the rest of your program.

Revision Questions for Section Two

Well, that just about wraps up the programming section, perfect time to try some revision questions I think.

- Try these questions and <u>tick off each one</u> when you <u>get it right</u>.
- When you've done <u>all the questions</u> for a topic and are <u>completely happy</u> with it, tick off the topic.

Data Types, Operators, Constants, Variables and Strings (p8-11) ☐

1) Define the following data types: integer, real, boolean, character and string.

2)* Write a piece of pseudo-code that converts:
   - a) the string '1234' into an integer.
   - b) the real 0.578 into a string.
   - c) the integer 8 into a string.
   - d) the string '0.75' into a real.

3) In pseudo-code, what do each of these operators do?
   - a) =
   - b) MOD
   - c) *
   - d) ←
   - e) DIV

4) What is meant by: a) a constant?   b) a variable?

5) a) Define string concatenation and give an example of it being used.
   b)* What will each of the following pieces of pseudo-code return if colour ← 'magenta'?
      - (i) LEN(colour)
      - (ii) POSITION(colour, 'g')
      - (iii) SUBSTRING(0, 3, colour)

Program Flow, Boolean Operators and Random Numbers (p12-17) ☐

6) In 20 words or less, outline what each of these statements does:
   - a) IF statement
   - b) CASE statement.

7) What is the main difference between ELSE-IF statements and nested IF statements?

8) Compare the features of the three condition-controlled loops, REPEAT-UNTIL, WHILE and DO-WHILE.

9)* Write an algorithm that outputs the number of Mondays in a 30-day month when the user inputs the day of the week that the month started on.

10)* Write an algorithm to simulate 100 rolls of an 8-sided dice and output the result of each roll.

Arrays, Records and File Handling (p18-21) ☐

11) Why are arrays useful?

12)* Write commands to perform the following operations on this array. The name of the array is 'chars'.
    ['3', 'T', 'P', '2', 'M', 'e', '4', 'q', 's', '3'].
    - a) Output the character 'M'.
    - b) Replace the 'P' in the chars array with a 'D'.
    - c) Replace every element in the chars array with an 'N'.

13)* Write an algorithm to create a two-dimensional array with 10 rows and 10 columns where each element is an integer and its value is given by the row number multiplied by the column number.
    (Hint: Remember that rows and columns are numbered starting at 0.)

14) In programming, data can be stored in records:
    - a) What is a record?
    - b) Give two differences between a record and a field.

15) Give one benefit of storing data in an external file.

16) Briefly describe what each of the following functions do:
    - a) OPEN()
    - b) CLOSE()
    - c) WRITELINE()
    - d) READLINE()

Subroutines (p22-23) ☐

17) What is a subroutine?

18) What is the difference between a function and a procedure?

19) Define these terms: a) parameter   b) local variable   c) global variable

*Answers on p73

Structured Programming

On p22-23 you saw how subroutines could be used to store a whole set of instructions under one name. Well, a single program will typically use lots of subroutines that each perform specific and simple tasks.

Structured Programming makes Coding much Easier

1) <u>Structured</u> (or modular) programming involves <u>decomposing</u> (see p1) the program that you want to write into <u>manageable modules</u>. Each of those <u>modules</u> is then decomposed even further into <u>smaller modules</u> and eventually into modules that perform <u>individual tasks</u>.

2) Simple <u>subroutines</u> can be written to carry out each individual task. Then the <u>bigger modules</u> and <u>main program</u> can be written using these <u>subroutines</u>.

3) It's important to clearly document the <u>interface</u> of each module. This means listing the module's <u>name</u>, any <u>inputs</u> (i.e. parameters), <u>processes</u> (what the module does) and the <u>output</u>/<u>return value</u> (if any).

4) For example, to design a program simulating a game of noughts and crosses you might have:

Program module design

Noughts and Crosses Program
— Set up a new game
— Play the game
— Work out winner
— Reset the program

Set up a new game:
— Enter player names
— Enter number of rounds
— Choose who goes first

Module interface for setting up a new game

Module	Input(s)	Process	Return Value
Enter player names	None	Prompt user for two names	Array of player names
Enter number of rounds	None	Prompt user for a number of rounds	Number of rounds
Choose who goes first	Array of player names	Randomly select a name	Name of player going first

The output of one module is often the input of another.

ADVANTAGES OF STRUCTURED PROGRAMMING

• Coding is <u>easier</u> because you're only writing subroutines that carry out very <u>simple tasks</u>.

• Lots of programmers can work on one program as each module can be written <u>independently</u>.

• It's <u>easier to test</u> structured programs as each module can be <u>tested individually</u> (see p27).

• Individual subroutines and modules can be <u>fixed</u> and <u>updated without affecting</u> the rest of the program.

• You will be able to <u>reuse</u> the subroutines and modules in programs you write <u>in the future</u>.

Your program should be Easy To Maintain

1) When using structured programming, it's important that your code is <u>well-maintained</u>.

2) A well-maintained program makes it <u>easy</u> for other programmers to understand what the code does. They should also be able to <u>change</u> parts of the source code without the risk of causing problems elsewhere in the code (e.g. knock on effects).

3) The following features can <u>improve</u> the maintainability of source code:

• <u>Comments</u> (usually written after # or //) are useful for <u>explaining</u> what the <u>key features</u> of a program do — <u>well written</u> and <u>clear</u> comments are fundamental for helping other programmers <u>understand your programs</u>.

Too many comments can leave your programs looking <u>cluttered</u> and <u>unreadable</u>.

• <u>Indentation</u> can be used to separate <u>different statements</u> in a program. This allows other programmers to see the flow of the program more <u>clearly</u> and pick out the <u>different features</u>.

• <u>Variables</u>, <u>subroutines</u> and <u>parameters</u> should be named so that they refer to what they actually are. This helps programmers to understand what they do, and makes it easier to <u>keep track</u> of them.

• Only use <u>global variables</u> (see p23) when <u>necessary</u> as they could affect the rest of your code. Variables with a <u>local scope</u> will only affect the subroutines that they are <u>declared in</u> — other programmers will know that <u>changing these variables</u> won't affect <u>other parts</u> of the program.

Look after your programs and they will look after you...

The key to a well-structured program is plenty of planning — decomposing the program into modules is always the first step. Have a go at finishing off the design for the noughts and crosses program above.

Authentication and Validation

Authentication and validation are used to improve the security and robustness of your programs.

Authentication can help Protect your programs

1) <u>Authentication</u> can <u>confirm the identity</u> of a user before they're allowed to access certain pieces of data or features of the program. A common way that programs do this is using <u>passwords</u>.

2) <u>Passwords</u> are usually associated with a <u>username</u>. When someone tries to access a protected part of the program, it should ask them for their password to check that they are who they claim to be.

3) Here are some common ways to <u>increase the security</u> of a password-based authentication system:

- Force users to use <u>strong passwords</u> (p64) and get them to change their passwords <u>regularly</u>.
- Limit the number of <u>failed authentication attempts</u> before access to an account is lost.
- Ask for a <u>random selection of characters</u> from the password on each authentication.

4) It's important that programmers get the <u>level of authentication</u> correct — too much authentication can affect a program's <u>functionality</u> and put people off using it.

5) A typical <u>authentication routine</u> will follow this structure:

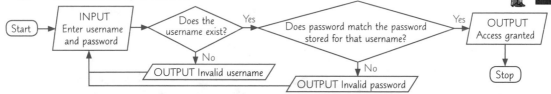

Validation can make sure the Inputs can't be Exploited

1) The easiest way for a user to <u>accidentally</u> or <u>intentionally misuse</u> a program is when entering data. You can try to prevent this from happening by using <u>validation</u>.

> **INPUT VALIDATION** — checking if data meets <u>certain criteria</u> before passing it into the program.
> E.g. checking that an email address contains an @ symbol and has a suitable ending (.com, .co.uk, etc).

2) Here are a few common types of <u>input validation check</u> you can use:

Range check	Checks the data is within a <u>specified range</u>.
Presence check	Checks the data has actually been <u>entered</u>.
Format check	Checks the data has the <u>correct format</u> (e.g. a date).
Look-up table	Checks the data against a table of <u>acceptable values</u>.
Length check	Checks the data is the <u>correct length</u>.

EXAMPLE:

Karen wants to validate usernames for an online forum. She wants each username to be longer than 5 characters, shorter than 12 characters and start with an uppercase letter.

a) Give two validation checks Karen would need to use.
- Length check to make sure the username is not longer or shorter than the lengths allowed.
- Format check to make sure the username starts with an uppercase letter.

b) Write a subroutine that will check if a username is a valid length.

```
SUBROUTINE validateUsername(username)
    usernameLength ← LEN(username)
    IF usernameLength > 5 AND usernameLength < 12 THEN
        RETURN true
    ELSE
        RETURN false
    ENDIF
ENDSUBROUTINE
```

I'm taking my wife hiking at the weekend — it's our first validate...

You should be able to write subroutines to perform simple authentication and validation checks.
Think about who you want to access your programs and what data you want them to be able to enter.

Testing

When you're writing programs, remember that the testing is just as important as the programming itself. Have a look at this page to test your knowledge of testing — they'll prepare you for being tested in the tests.

Programming Errors can be Syntax Errors and Logic Errors

1) It's quite typical for a program to contain <u>errors</u> during its development — these errors need to be <u>found</u> and <u>corrected</u> as soon as possible.

2) The first task is to figure out what <u>type of error</u> has occurred:

@ triangel has 3 sides?!

> SYNTAX ERRORS — when the compiler or interpreter <u>doesn't understand</u> something you've typed because it doesn't follow the <u>rules</u> or <u>grammar</u> of the programming language.
>
> LOGIC ERRORS — when the compiler or interpreter is able to <u>run the program</u>, but the program does something <u>unexpected</u>.

3) <u>Syntax errors</u> can be <u>diagnosed</u> by compilers and interpreters (see p29) — they'll be unable to turn the <u>source code</u> into <u>machine code</u> and a syntax error (with its location) will be returned.

4) <u>Logic errors</u> are more <u>difficult to diagnose</u> and <u>track down</u> — compilers and interpreters <u>won't</u> pick them up. Logic errors are found through general use of the program and by systematically <u>testing</u> it using a <u>test plan</u> (see below).

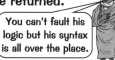
You can't fault his logic but his syntax is all over the place.

A Test Plan should be made Before Implementation

1) A <u>test plan</u> will outline exactly what you're going to test and how you're going to test it. It should cover all the <u>possible paths</u> through a program.

Possible paths are all the branches of the flowchart (p3) for your program.

2) A <u>good test plan</u> will anticipate potential issues with the program and select appropriate <u>test data</u> to test for these issues.

3) The <u>test data</u> that you use in your test plan should fall into one of three categories:

- <u>Normal (typical) data</u> — things that a user is <u>likely</u> to input into the program.
- <u>Boundary (extreme) data</u> — values at the <u>limit</u> of what the program should be able to handle.
- <u>Erroneous data</u> — inputs that the program <u>should not accept</u>.

Extreme enough for ya?

4) The table below shows an example of a test plan for setting an alarm system. Users should be able to set their own 3-5 digit alarm code.

Type of data	Test data	Reason for testing	Expected outcome
Normal	2476	To see how the alarm copes with normal usage.	Code accepted.
Normal	No input	To see if the alarm prompts an input.	Prompt to enter a code.
Boundary	000	To see if the smallest code is accepted.	Code accepted.
Boundary	99999	To see if the largest code is accepted.	Code accepted.
Erroneous	23aY	To see if the system accepts non-digits.	Error: The code contains non-numeric data.
Erroneous	12	To see if the alarm accepts fewer than 3-digit inputs.	Error: The code is too short.
Erroneous	632191	To see if the alarm accepts more than 5-digit inputs.	Error: The code is too long.

5) During testing, the tester can add "<u>actual outcome</u>" and "<u>pass or fail</u>" columns to the table.

6) <u>Trace tables</u> (see p28) can be used when you've <u>identified</u> that there is a logic error. They will help you <u>trace the values</u> that the variables take as you go through the program so you can <u>pin-point exactly</u> where something has <u>gone wrong</u>.

Sorry, this page is still in the testing stage... Error 50: Line is too long!

When it comes to your exams you'll need to be able to choose suitable test data for a given program — remember that you'll need to choose normal, boundary and erroneous data. A handy tip is to think "How could I ruin the programmer's day by breaking their beloved program?" and you'll be all set.

Trace Tables and Time Efficiency

Trace tables will be your best friend when you're learning the fundamentals of programming. They help you to follow a piece of code in a systematic way to see if it's behaving itself or if it's up to no good.

Trace Tables help you to find Logic Errors

1) <u>Trace tables</u> give a simple way of testing that a piece of code is <u>working correctly</u>. They <u>keep track</u> of the <u>values</u> that <u>certain variables</u> take as you go through the code.

2) Their main use is to '<u>dry run</u>' a subroutine or algorithm to make sure there are <u>no logic errors</u> — they can also be used to help you figure out what a piece of code is actually doing.

3) The <u>columns</u> of a trace table usually represent <u>variables</u>. Each <u>row</u> of a trace table represents the <u>values</u> that the variables take at a <u>particular point</u> in the algorithm.

EXAMPLE: The subroutine on the right is used to add up all of the odd numbers up to the given number. Complete the trace table below when the subroutine call sumOfOdd(5) is made.

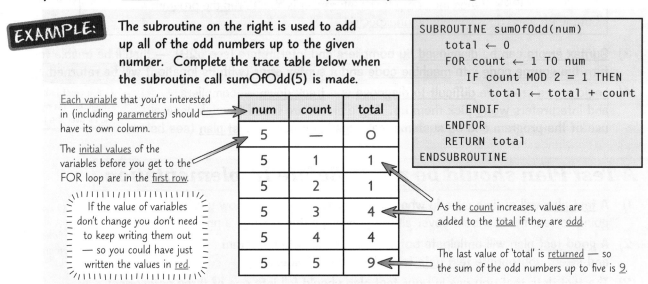

```
SUBROUTINE sumOfOdd(num)
    total ← 0
    FOR count ← 1 TO num
        IF count MOD 2 = 1 THEN
            total ← total + count
        ENDIF
    ENDFOR
    RETURN total
ENDSUBROUTINE
```

Each variable that you're interested in (including parameters) should have its own column.

The initial values of the variables before you get to the FOR loop are in the first row.

If the value of variables don't change you don't need to keep writing them out — so you could have just written the values in red.

num	count	total
5	—	0
5	1	1
5	2	1
5	3	4
5	4	4
5	5	9

As the count increases, values are added to the total if they are odd.

The last value of 'total' is returned — so the sum of the odd numbers up to five is 9.

4) The <u>columns</u> of a trace table might not always be variables — they could be any information that the programmer is <u>interested in</u>. For example, they might have a column for the length of an array or for the output of the algorithm.

5) When testing a <u>larger program</u>, the tester will often use <u>debugging tools</u> — for example, breakpoints are used to stop the program at certain places so that you can look at the values of variables.

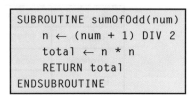

Table tracing attempt #9

Algorithms are also tested for Time Efficiency

1) Many <u>different algorithms</u> can be constructed to perform the <u>same task</u> (e.g. the searching and sorting algorithms on p4-6).

2) Each algorithm will take a certain amount of '<u>time</u>' to complete the task. Algorithms that take <u>less 'time'</u> to complete a task are said to have a <u>better time efficiency</u>.

3) When programmers talk about the amount of 'time' an algorithm takes, they usually don't measure the <u>real-life time</u>. They measure things like the number of times <u>memory was accessed</u>, the number of <u>CPU cycles</u> taken to <u>execute commands</u> or the number of times a <u>loop was executed</u>.

```
SUBROUTINE sumOfOdd(num)
    n ← (num + 1) DIV 2
    total ← n * n
    RETURN total
ENDSUBROUTINE
```

This subroutine does exactly the same as the one above but it doesn't have a loop. For large values of the parameter this algorithm would have a much better time efficiency.

Programmers are often interested in the <u>space efficiency</u> of an algorithm too — this is the amount of space in memory that an algorithm uses.

How many times did you access memory on that page?

Time efficient revision isn't always best — sometimes you just need to keep looping through a page until you remember it. If trace tables crop up in your exam, you might not be told the purpose of the algorithm you're tracing — don't worry, just work your way through the algorithm pretending you're a computer.

Translators

For computers to process any computer language it needs to be translated into machine code.

Computer Languages can be High-Level or Low-Level

1) Most of the programming languages that you'll be familiar with (e.g. Python, C++) are high-level languages. The source code is easy for humans to write, but computers need to translate it into machine code before they can read and run it.

2) On the other hand, low-level languages are tricky for humans to read and write but are easier for a computer to run. They consist of machine code and assembly languages:

```
000000 00010 00011 00100 00000 100000
```
← Machine code is very tricky for humans to understand. Each processor (or family of processors) will have its own specific machine code.

Assembly code is more readable for humans and easier to remember, so programmers are less likely
```
ADD r4, r2, r3
```
← to make mistakes writing assembly code than machine code. It's often used when developing software for embedded systems (see p46) and when programmers need more control over specific hardware.

3) High-level languages are popular with programmers, but low-level languages have their uses too:

High-Level Languages	Low-Level Languages
• One instruction of high-level code represents many instructions of machine code.	• One instruction of assembly code usually only represents one instruction of machine code.
• The same code will work for many different machines and processors.	• Usually written for one type of machine or processor and won't work on any others.
• The programmer can easily store data in lots of different structures (e.g. lists and arrays) without knowing about the memory structure.	• The programmer needs to know about the internal structure of the CPU (see p47-48) and how it manages the memory.
• Code is easy to read, understand and modify.	• Code is very difficult to read, understand and modify.
• Must be translated into machine code before a computer is able to understand it.	• Commands in machine code can be executed directly without the need for a translator.
• You don't have much control over what the CPU actually does so programs will be less memory efficient and slower.	• You control exactly what the CPU does and how it uses memory so programs will be more memory efficient and faster.

Translators convert programming languages into Machine Code

1) Computers only understand instructions given to them as machine code, so high level languages and assembly languages need to be translated before a computer is able to execute the instructions.

2) There are three types of translator that you need to know about: assemblers, compilers and interpreters.

3) Assemblers are used to turn assembly language into machine code. There are many different assembly languages (to support different CPU types) and each one needs its own unique assembler.

4) Compilers and interpreters are both used to turn high-level code into machine code.

Compiler	Interpreter
Translates all of the source code at the same time and creates one executable file.	Translates and runs the source code one instruction at a time, but doesn't create an executable file.
Only needed once to create the executable file.	Needed every time you want to run the program.
Returns a list of errors for the entire program once compiling is complete.	The interpreter will return the first error it finds and then stop — this is useful for debugging.
Once compiled the program runs quickly, but compiling can take a long time.	Programs will run more slowly because the code is being translated as the program is running.

5) The type of translator used will often be influenced by the programming language you're using.

6) However, sometimes programmers want to use a specific type of translator — interpreters are often used when you're developing software and compilers when you want to distribute software.

"Cette page est incroyable!" — call in the translators...

This page just screams for an exam question on comparing languages or translators. You should know the key features of low-level languages, high-level languages, assemblers, compilers and interpreters.

Revision Questions for Section Three

And just like that it's the end of <u>section three</u> — but before you put the book down, you've got one more task.
- Try these questions and <u>tick off each one</u> when you <u>get it right</u>.
- When you've done <u>all the questions</u> for a topic and are <u>completely happy</u> with it, tick off the topic.

Structured Programming (p25) ☑

1) What is structured programming?

2) Give five advantages of using structured programming.

3) a) Give four features of maintainable source code.
   b) Explain how each feature can help other programmers to maintain your code.

Authentication and Validation (p26) ☑

4) What is authentication and why is it used?

5) Give three things that can be done to make a password-based authentication system more secure.

6) Draw a flowchart to show a standard username and password authentication routine.

7) Define the term input validation.

8) Give five types of input validation check and explain what each check does.

9)* The program below checks which year the user was born in.
   What type of input validation check does it use? Explain your answer.

```
REPEAT
    OUTPUT 'Enter the year you were born'
    year ← USERINPUT
UNTIL year > 1900 AND year <= 2016
```

Testing, Trace Tables and Time Efficiency (p27-28) ☑

10) Define the following terms: a) Syntax Error   b) Logic Error

11) Explain why logic errors are more difficult to diagnose than syntax errors.

12) What are the three different types of test data?

13)* A software company is designing an anagram application. It will take a string
   of letters and return all of the words that can be spelt using all of the letters exactly once.
   Come up with five pieces of test data that the company could use to test their program.

14) What are trace tables used for?

15)* Complete the trace table for
   the algorithm given on the right.
   You may need to add more rows.

```
arr ← [2, 5, 1, 2, 3]
total ← 1
FOR x ←0 TO LEN(arr)-1
    total ← total * arr[x]
ENDFOR
OUTPUT total
```

x	arr[x]	total

16) Describe what time efficiency is in the most time efficient way possible.

Translators (p29) ☑

17) Define and give an example of the following: a) Machine code   b) Assembly Language

18) Give six differences between high-level languages and low-level languages.

19) What are the three types of translator?

20) Compare the functionality and uses of a compiler and an interpreter.

*Answers on p73

Logic

Logic gates are pretty clever stuff. They take binary information and give an output based on the Boolean operations (p16). Each Boolean operator (<u>NOT</u>, <u>AND</u> and <u>OR</u>) has its own logic gate.

Logic Gates apply Boolean Operations to Inputs

1) Logic gates are special circuits built into computer chips.
   They receive <u>binary data</u>, apply a <u>Boolean operation</u>, then <u>output</u> a binary result.

2) Logic <u>diagrams</u> are often drawn to show logic gates and circuits.
   Each type of logic gate is shown by a different <u>symbol</u>.

3) Each type of logic gate also has a corresponding <u>truth table</u>.
   Truth tables show <u>all</u> possible input combinations of 1s and 0s, and the corresponding <u>outputs</u>.

NOT gate

1) NOT gates take a <u>single input</u> and give a <u>single output</u>.

2) The output is always the <u>opposite</u> value to the input.
   If <u>1</u> is input, it outputs <u>0</u>. If <u>0</u> is input, it outputs <u>1</u>.

It can help to think of 1s as TRUE and 0s as FALSE.

<u>NOT gate symbol</u>

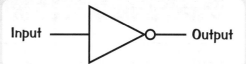

Input ———▷o——— Output

<u>NOT truth table</u>

Input	Output
0	1
1	0

AND gate

1) AND gates take <u>two inputs</u> and give <u>one output</u>.

2) If both inputs are 1, the output is <u>1</u>,
   <u>otherwise</u> the output is <u>0</u>.

<u>AND gate symbol</u>

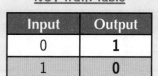

Input A ———
)——— Output
Input B ———

<u>AND truth table</u>

Input A	Input B	Output
0	0	0
0	1	0
1	0	0
1	1	1

OR gate

1) OR gates take <u>two inputs</u> and give <u>one output</u>.

2) If <u>one or more</u> inputs are 1, then the output is <u>1</u>,
   <u>otherwise</u> the output is <u>0</u>.

<u>OR gate symbol</u>

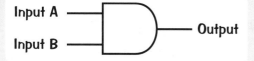

Input A ———
)——— Output
Input B ———

<u>OR truth table</u>

Input A	Input B	Output
0	0	0
0	1	1
1	0	1
1	1	1

Logic isn't as scary as it looks...

These basic logic gates are the building blocks for bigger logic circuits —
you should be able to draw each logic gate and the corresponding truth table.
You might also see the symbols shown in this table as equivalent notation:

Gate	Expression	Notation
NOT	NOT A	¬A
AND	A AND B	A ∧ B
OR	A OR B	A ∨ B

Logic

You can make more interesting logic diagrams by <u>combining</u> logic gates. If you know the truth tables from the previous page you'll be able to create truth tables for much more complicated logic diagrams.

Logic Gates are Combined for More Complex Operations

1) <u>Multiple</u> logic gates can be added to the <u>same</u> logic circuit to carry out different operations.

2) You can work out the <u>truth tables</u> by working through each gate in order.
   For every <u>input</u> combination, follow them through each gate <u>step-by-step</u>, then write down the <u>output</u>.

3) By using brackets and the terms AND, OR and NOT, circuits can be written as <u>logical statements</u>, like NOT(A AND B) below. Operations in <u>brackets</u> should be completed <u>first</u>, just like in normal maths.

This circuit shows <u>AND</u> followed by <u>NOT</u>.

The <u>truth table</u> looks like this:

A	B	A AND B	P = NOT(A AND B)
0	0	0	1
0	1	0	1
1	0	0	1
1	1	1	0

This circuit shows <u>OR</u> followed by <u>NOT</u>.

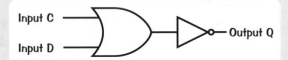

The <u>truth table</u> looks like this:

C	D	C OR D	Q = NOT(C OR D)
0	0	0	1
0	1	1	0
1	0	1	0
1	1	1	0

4) The two logic circuits shown above are examples of <u>two-level logic circuits</u> — they require the inputs to pass through a <u>maximum</u> of <u>two</u> logic gates to reach the output.

Logic Circuits can have More than Two Inputs

This is a <u>two-level logic</u> circuit with <u>3 inputs</u>.

Using Boolean operators, this circuit can be written as <u>R = (A OR B) AND (NOT C)</u>. (This is an example of <u>Boolean algebra</u>).

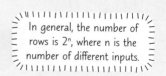

To cover <u>every</u> input combination, extra rows are needed in the truth table. There are <u>3</u> inputs and each can take one of 2 values, so $2 \times 2 \times 2 = \underline{8}$ rows are needed.

In general, the number of rows is 2^n, where n is the number of different inputs.

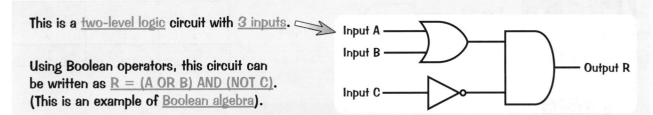

A	B	C	A OR B	NOT C	R = (A OR B) AND (NOT C)
0	0	0	0	1	0
0	0	1	0	0	0
0	1	0	1	1	1
0	1	1	1	0	0
1	0	0	1	1	1
1	0	1	1	0	0
1	1	0	1	1	1
1	1	1	1	0	0

To be OR NOT to be — literally covering all forms of being...

Once you've learned each gate's truth table, you can work out the truth tables of much more complicated circuits. If you take the inputs through each gate one step at a time you'll be fine — it's only logical...

Units

Just like you have units like centimetres, metres and kilometres for measuring distance, computers need units for measuring <u>digital information</u>. It looks like whoever came up with them was really hungry at the time...

Bits are the Smallest Measure of Data

1) Computers use 1s and 0s to represent the flow of electricity.
<u>1</u> is used to show that electricity <u>is</u> flowing, and <u>0</u> shows that it is <u>not</u> flowing.

2) All the data we want a computer to process must be converted into <u>binary code</u> (1s and 0s).

3) Each 1 or 0 in a binary code is a <u>bit</u> (<u>bi</u>nary dig<u>it</u>). For example, 1010 is 4 bits.

4) The table below shows <u>the size</u> of other units of data:

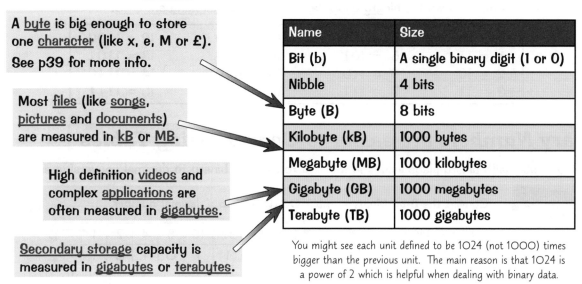

A <u>byte</u> is big enough to store one <u>character</u> (like x, e, M or £). See p39 for more info.

Most <u>files</u> (like <u>songs</u>, <u>pictures</u> and <u>documents</u>) are measured in <u>kB</u> or <u>MB</u>.

High definition <u>videos</u> and complex <u>applications</u> are often measured in <u>gigabytes</u>.

<u>Secondary storage</u> capacity is measured in <u>gigabytes</u> or <u>terabytes</u>.

Name	Size
Bit (b)	A single binary digit (1 or 0)
Nibble	4 bits
Byte (B)	8 bits
Kilobyte (kB)	1000 bytes
Megabyte (MB)	1000 kilobytes
Gigabyte (GB)	1000 megabytes
Terabyte (TB)	1000 gigabytes

You might see each unit defined to be 1024 (not 1000) times bigger than the previous unit. The main reason is that 1024 is a power of 2 which is helpful when dealing with binary data.

5) Each <u>bit</u> can take one of <u>two different values</u> (either 1 or 0). This means that a <u>nibble</u> (4 bits) can take $2^4 = $ <u>16 different values</u>, and a <u>byte</u> (8 bits) can take $2^8 = $ <u>256 different values</u>.

You can Convert between Different Units

<u>Converting</u> between units of data is usually pretty straightforward — just watch out when you have to switch between <u>bits</u> and <u>bytes</u>.

EXAMPLE: Ashley has downloaded some images to her computer. Each image is 300 kilobytes.

a) How many bits are in each image?

1) First, convert to bytes by <u>multiplying by 1000</u>: 300 kB = 300 × 1000 = 300 000 Bytes

2) There are 8 bits in a byte, so <u>multiply by 8</u>: 300 000 Bytes = 300 000 × 8
   = 2 400 000 bits

b) She wants to copy 400 of these images onto her USB flash drive, which has 0.15 GB of free space left. Does she have enough space to store them all?

1) Work out the <u>total size</u> of all the images: 400 × 300 = 120 000 kB

2) Now convert this to GB — first, <u>divide by 1000</u> to get it in MB, then <u>again</u> to get it in GB: 120 000 kB = 120 000 ÷ 1000 = 120 MB
   120 MB = 120 ÷ 1000 = 0.12 GB

So yes, she has enough space.

This page has me in bits...

Keep working your way through that unit table until the size order is clear in your head — it might just show up on your exam. A bit is smaller than a nibble, and a nibble is less than a full byte. I know, hilarious.

Binary Numbers

As computers only understand 1s and 0s, all data must be converted into binary to be processed. Binary can be used to represent all numbers in our standard number system.

Counting in Binary is a bit like Counting in Decimal

1) In our standard number system we have ten different digits (0, 1, 2, 3, 4, 5, 6, 7, 8, 9). This is called <u>decimal</u>, <u>denary</u> or <u>base-10</u>.

2) <u>Binary</u> only uses <u>two</u> different digits (0 and 1) — we call this <u>base-2</u>.

3) Counting in binary is similar to counting in decimal, but the place values from <u>right</u> to <u>left</u> increase by <u>powers of 2</u> (e.g. 8, 4, 2, 1), instead of powers of 10 (e.g. 1000, 100, 10, 1).

4) The following table shows the <u>binary equivalents</u> of the <u>decimal numbers 0-15</u>:

0 = 0	4 = 100	8 = 1000	12 = 1100
1 = 1	5 = 101	9 = 1001	13 = 1101
2 = 10	6 = 110	10 = 1010	14 = 1110
3 = 11	7 = 111	11 = 1011	15 = 1111

Binary Numbers are easier to Convert using Tables

Drawing a table with binary <u>place values</u> in the first row makes binary to decimal conversion easier.

EXAMPLE: Convert the 8-bit binary number 0011 0101 to a decimal number.

Each column is just a power of 2. i.e. 2^3, 2^2, 2^1, 2^0.

1) Draw up a table with binary place values in the top row. Start with 1 at the right, then move left, doubling each time.

128	64	32	16	8	4	2	1
0	0	1	1	0	1	0	1

2) Write the binary number 0011 0101 into your table.

3) Add up all the numbers with a 1 in their column: 32 + 16 + 4 + 1 = 53

So 0011 0101 is 53 in decimal.

This works with all binary numbers — just draw as many columns as you need, doubling each time.

<u>8-bit</u> numbers can represent the decimal numbers 0 to 255. <u>16-bit</u> numbers can show the numbers 0 to 65 535, and <u>32-bit</u> can show the numbers 0 to 4 294 967 295.

Convert Decimal to Binary by Subtracting

When converting from <u>decimal</u> to <u>binary</u>, it's easier to draw a <u>table</u> of binary place values, then <u>subtract them</u> from <u>largest</u> to <u>smallest</u>. Have a look at this example:

EXAMPLE: Convert the decimal number 79 into an 8-bit binary number.

1) Draw an 8-bit table.

128	64	32	16	8	4	2	1
0	1	0	0	1	1	1	1

2) Move along the table, <u>only</u> subtracting the number in each column from your <u>running total</u> if it gives a <u>positive</u> answer.

3) Put a 1 in every column that gives a positive answer, and a 0 in the rest.

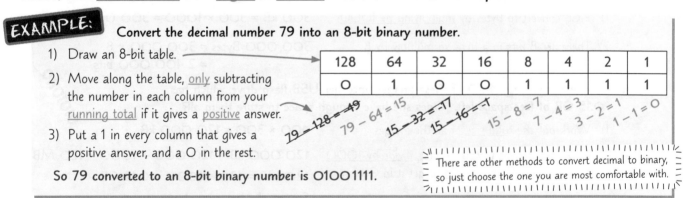

79 − 128 = 49   79 − 64 = 15   15 − 32 = −17   15 − 16 = −1   15 − 8 = 7   7 − 4 = 3   3 − 2 = 1   1 − 1 = 0

So 79 converted to an 8-bit binary number is 0100 1111.

There are other methods to convert decimal to binary, so just choose the one you are most comfortable with.

Why was 110 afraid of 111? Because 111 1000 1001...

There are a couple of different conversions on this page, and you'll need to be comfortable with it all before carrying on. Remember that to read each digit from smallest to largest, read from right to left like with decimal numbers. The value of each digit in binary is double the value of the digit to its right.

Binary Numbers

More binary numbers coming right up, hope you're ready for another page full of 0s and 1s. Adding binary numbers is a lot like adding decimal numbers — have a look at this page of examples to see how it's done...

Add Binary Numbers using Column Addition

As binary only uses 1s and 0s we <u>can</u> comfortably do 0 + 0 = 0, 1 + 0 = 1 and 0 + 1 = 1.

Using binary we <u>can't</u> write 1 + 1 = 2. Instead, we have to write <u>1 + 1 = 10</u>.

EXAMPLES: **1.** Add the following 8-bit binary numbers together: 10001101 and 01001000

1) First, put the binary numbers into <u>columns</u>.

2) Starting from the <u>right</u>, add the numbers in columns.

3) When doing <u>1 + 1 = 10</u>, carry the 1 into the next column.

So 10001101 + 01001000 = 11010101

```
    1 0 0 0 1 1 0 1
+   0 1 0 0 1 0 0 0
  ─────────────────
    1 1 0 1 0 1 0 1
                  1
```

You can add <u>more binary numbers</u> together at the same time just be careful when you get 1 + 1 + 1...

2. Calculate the sum of the binary numbers 01001011, 10001001 and 00100101.

```
    0 1 0 0 1 0 1 1
    1 0 0 0 1 0 0 1
+   0 0 1 0 0 1 0 1
  ─────────────────
    1 1 1 1 1 0 0 1
        1 1 1 1
```

1) Put the numbers in <u>columns</u> and add from the <u>right</u> like before.

2) Sometimes you'll get something like <u>1 + 1 + 1 = 11</u>, so you need to write 1, then carry 1 to the next column.

So 01001011 + 10001001 + 00100101 = 11111001

```
1 + 0 = 1
0 + 1 = 1
1 + 1 = 10
1 + 1 + 1 = 11
```

You can add binary numbers with <u>different numbers of bits</u> — just <u>add some 0s</u> to the <u>front</u> of the numbers with fewer bits.

3. Calculate the sum of the binary numbers 110011, 1101001 and 10110

1) <u>Add zeros</u> to the front of 110011 and 10110 so that all the numbers have <u>7-bits</u>.

2) Add up the numbers in the normal way.

3) The answer has <u>8-bits</u>.

So 110011 + 1101001 + 10110 = 10110010

```
    0 1 1 0 0 1 1
    1 1 0 1 0 0 1
+   0 0 1 0 1 1 0
  ───────────────
  1 0 1 1 0 0 1 0
    1 1 1 1 1 1 1
```

You can <u>check your answers</u> to binary addition by converting the numbers and answer to <u>decimal</u>, to make sure it still works. For example 3 above:

110011 = 51   1101001 = 105

10110 = 22   10110010 = 178

51 + 105 + 22 = 178 so the answer is correct.

Binary Benefit #1010 — 10 Green Bottles is much shorter...

Okay so that was a lot of examples just adding binary numbers together, but the best way to learn how to do it is practice, practice and more practice. You can test yourself by writing down two or three random binary numbers and adding them together, then check your answer by converting it all to decimal.

Binary Numbers

Computers have a few tricks to help them do tough calculations — one of these tricks is using binary shifts...

Binary Shifts can be used to Multiply or Divide by 2

1) A binary shift (also known as a logical shift) moves every bit in a binary number left or right a certain number of places.

2) Gaps at the beginning or end of the number are filled in with 0s.

3) The direction of the binary shift indicates whether it multiplies or divides the binary number:

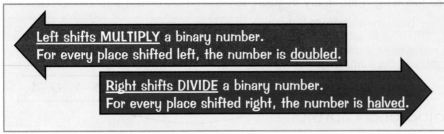

Forget manual gears mate. Everyone drives binary shift these days.

Left shifts MULTIPLY a binary number.
For every place shifted left, the number is doubled.

Right shifts DIVIDE a binary number.
For every place shifted right, the number is halved.

4) If a number is shifted 3 places right, it would be halved three times (i.e. divided by $2^3 = 8$).
If a number were shifted 4 places left, it would be doubled four times (i.e. multiplied by $2^4 = 16$).

5) If you're only working with 8-bit numbers, binary shifts can cause 1s to 'drop off' the end.
Losing 1s in a left shift will give a very different answer to the multiplication (see below).
Losing 1s in a right shift will give an inaccurate answer (rounded down to the nearest whole number).

Examples of Binary Shifts

EXAMPLE:

Perform a 3 place left shift on the 8-bit binary number 00101001.
Explain the effect this will have on the number and problems that may occur.

| 0 | 0 | 1 | 0 | 1 | 0 | 0 | 1 |

| 0 | 0 | 1 | 0 | 1 | 0 | 0 | 1 | 0 | 0 | 0 |

1) Write down the original binary number, then shift all digits 3 places to the left.

2) Fill in the gaps on the right with 0s.
The number has been doubled three times, so it has been multiplied by $2^3 = 8$.

If there are only 8 bits available to store the number, then a 1 will drop off the end — this will make the answer to the calculation wrong.

In decimal, this is 41 × 8 = 328, but the 8-bit answer is 72.

EXAMPLE:

Perform a 2 place right shift on the binary number 00111100.
What effect will this have on the number?

1) Write down the original binary number, then shift all digits 2 places to the right.

2) Fill in the gaps on the left with 0s.

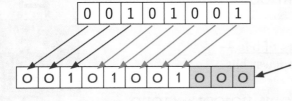

| 0 | 0 | 1 | 1 | 1 | 1 | 0 | 0 |

| 0 | 0 | 0 | 0 | 1 | 1 | 1 | 1 | X | X |

A 2 place right shift gives the binary number 00001111.
As this is a 2 place shift, the original number
will have been halved twice (so divided by $2^2 = 4$).

Dividing using a right binary shift has the same effect as using the DIV operator (p9) — your answer would not take into account any remainders.

It's just a shift to the left (and then a shift to the riiiiiiiiiiiiiiiiiiiiiight)...

Binary shifts are really good for doing super fast multiplication and division, but only by powers of 2.
If you're losing 1s on a right shift, your answer will be inaccurate (and on a left shift, it'll be way out).

Hexadecimal Numbers

Hexadecimal (hex) is another number system used regularly in programming.
Hex uses a combination of digits and letters in order to represent a number.

Hexadecimal numbers are Shorter than Binary

1) Hexadecimal (or base-16) uses sixteen different digits.

2) A single hex character can represent any decimal number from 0-15. To represent 0-15 in binary would require 4 bits (a nibble), so each hex character equates to a nibble in binary.

3) The table shows the decimal and binary value of each hex character.

4) Programmers often prefer hex when coding, because:

- It's simpler to remember large numbers in hex — they're far shorter than binary numbers.
- Due to hex numbers being shorter, there's less chance of input errors.
- It's easier to convert between binary and hex than binary and decimal.

Decimal	Hex	Binary	Decimal	Hex	Binary
0	0	0000	8	8	1000
1	1	0001	9	9	1001
2	2	0010	10	A	1010
3	3	0011	11	B	1011
4	4	0100	12	C	1100
5	5	0101	13	D	1101
6	6	0110	14	E	1110
7	7	0111	15	F	1111

Computers themselves do not use hex — they still have to convert everything to binary to process it.

Convert Hex to Decimal by Multiplying each Character

In hex, moving right to left, place values increase in powers of 16.

4096	256	16	1

To convert from hex to decimal, draw up a table, fill in the boxes, then multiply — just like in this example:

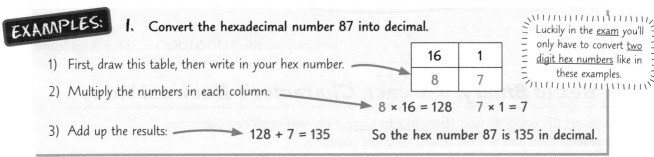

EXAMPLES: 1. Convert the hexadecimal number 87 into decimal.

1) First, draw this table, then write in your hex number.

16	1
8	7

Luckily in the exam you'll only have to convert two digit hex numbers like in these examples.

2) Multiply the numbers in each column.

8 × 16 = 128   7 × 1 = 7

3) Add up the results: → 128 + 7 = 135   So the hex number 87 is 135 in decimal.

To convert from decimal to hex, draw the table but use division to fill it in.

2. Convert the decimal number 106 into hexadecimal.

1) Start at the left. Divide 106 by 16, then hold onto the remainder.
106 ÷ 16 = 6 r 10

16	1
6	A

2) Divide the remainder from the last calculation by 1.
10 ÷ 1 = 10 = A

Remember, hex goes from 0-9, then A to F.

So the decimal number 106 is 6A in hexadecimal.

Hex can be a blessing and a curse...

Sometimes, hex and decimal can look fairly similar (as they both contain 0-9), so make sure you've got them the right way round when converting — 65 in hexadecimal is NOT the same as 65 in decimal.
Learn the hex table and its advantages, then cover it all up and write everything you can remember.

Hexadecimal Numbers

Convert Binary to Hex by splitting it into Nibbles

1) Each hex character is equal to a <u>nibble</u> in binary, so it is possible to convert from binary to hex by splitting the binary code into <u>4-bit chunks</u>.

2) Binary to hex conversions can be much <u>easier</u> than converting from binary to decimal, as you only have to deal with the nibbles <u>one at a time</u>.

Paul always eats food in 4-bit chunks. Get on with it, Paul.

EXAMPLE: Convert the binary number 10111001 to hexadecimal.

Remember, hex only uses letters for decimal values between 10-15.

1) Firstly, <u>split</u> the binary number into <u>nibbles</u>: 1011 1001

2) Draw a table with columns labelled 1, 2, 4, 8, then <u>repeat</u> the values for as many nibbles as you require.

3) Fill in the table with your binary number.

4) For <u>each nibble</u>, add up the numbers with a 1 in the column, then convert this value to hex.

5) Put the hex values <u>together</u>, and voila — you're done.

8	4	2	1	8	4	2	1
1	0	1	1	1	0	0	1

8 + 2 + 1 = 11   8 + 1 = <u>9</u>
= <u>B</u>

The binary number 10111001 is B9 in hexadecimal.

If the binary number can't be split into nibbles, you'll have to stick some zeros on the front.

EXAMPLE: Convert the binary number 1111101000 to hexadecimal.

1) Add <u>zeros</u> to the <u>front</u> of the binary number, so that you can split it into nibbles. → 0011 1110 1000

2) Draw a repeating table of 1, 2, 4 and 8, as above.

3) Write your binary number in the table.

4) Add up <u>each nibble</u> and <u>convert</u> each value to <u>hex</u>.

5) Put the hex values together.

8	4	2	1	8	4	2	1	8	4	2	1
0	0	1	1	1	1	1	0	1	0	0	0

2 + 1 = <u>3</u>   8 + 4 + 2 = 14   8 = <u>8</u>
= <u>E</u>

The binary number 1111101000 is 3E8 in hexadecimal.

For Hex to Binary, use each Character's Decimal Value

To convert the <u>opposite</u> way (from <u>hex</u> to <u>binary</u>) convert each hex character into binary, then just put the binary numbers together.

EXAMPLE: Convert the hexadecimal number 8C to binary.

1) First, find the decimal value of each character: 8 = 8 in decimal   C = 12 in decimal

2) Find the binary value of each decimal number:

8	4	2	1
1	0	0	0

8 = 1000 in binary

8	4	2	1
1	1	0	0

12 = 1100 in binary

3) Put the nibbles together to get the equivalent binary number.

The hexadecimal number 8C is 10001100 in binary.

This page has so many nibbles it could spoil your lunch...

The key with converting binary to hexadecimal is to split the binary up into chunks of 4 bits, each with columns labelled 1, 2, 4 and 8. Then work out the individual hex values and put them together.

Characters

Almost everything can be represented as binary code — words, images and sound can all be turned into bits and processed by a computer. Firstly let's look at words, which are made up of different characters.

Binary can be used to represent Characters

1) Alphanumeric characters are used to make words and strings (see p11). They include uppercase and lowercase letters, the digits 0-9, and symbols like ? + and £.

2) Computers are unable to process these characters directly as they only process binary code. So they need a way of converting these characters to binary code and vice versa. They can do this using character sets.

> Character sets are collections of characters that a computer recognises from their binary representation.

Don't mistake a character set for a font. A character set is what determines the letter — the font you use just displays that letter in a certain way.

3) As well as the alphanumeric characters mentioned above, character sets also contain special characters which do certain commands (e.g. space, enter and delete).

4) So when you press a button on your keyboard it sends a binary signal to the computer telling it which key you pressed. The computer then uses the character set to translate the binary code into a particular character.

The number of Bits you'll need is based on the Character Set

Different character sets can have different amounts of characters. The number of characters in a character set determines how many bits you'll need. Here are some standard character sets you should know about:

- **ASCII** is the most commonly-used character set in the English-speaking world. Each ASCII character is given a 7-bit binary code — this means it can represent a total of 128 different characters, including all the letters in the English alphabet, numbers, symbols and commands.

- An extra bit (0) is added to the start of the binary code for each ASCII character (see the table on the right). This means each ASCII character fits nicely into 1 byte.

- The codes for numbers, uppercase letters and lowercase letters are ordered (A comes before B comes before C...) with symbols and commands scattered around. E.g. From the table, the code for B is 66 in decimal. The code for E would be 3 after B, which is 66 + 3 = 69 in decimal or 0100 0101 in binary.

Character	Binary	Hex	Decimal
Backspace	0000 1000	8	8
0	0011 0000	30	48
1	0011 0001	31	49
=	0011 1101	3D	61
A	0100 0001	41	65
B	0100 0010	42	66
]	0101 1101	5D	93
a	0110 0001	61	97
b	0110 0010	62	98

Some examples of ASCII characters.

Extended ASCII uses 8-bit binary codes to represent 256 characters. The first 128 are the same as ASCII and the others are used for characters in other languages like French and German.

- **Unicode®** comes in several different forms and tries to cover every possible letter or symbol that might be written. Unlike ASCII, Unicode® uses multiple bytes for each character.

- The best thing about Unicode® is that it covers all major languages, even those that use a completely different alphabet like Greek, Russian and Chinese.

- The first 128 codes in Unicode® are the same as ASCII.

0001 0010   0110 1111
1011 0101   1001 1010

My computer started typing in Greek — it was out of character...

You don't need to remember the ASCII codes for any specific characters, but if you're given the ASCII code of one character (e.g. T) you should be able to work out the ASCII code for another character (e.g. W).

Storing Images

Images and sounds are pieces of data stored on computers — so, naturally, they're made of bits (p33). How those bits turn into your latest selfie or your favourite Jason-B song is covered on the next two pages.

Images are stored as a series of Pixels

1) The type of image you use most often is a bitmap — they're mainly used for photos. Bitmap images are made up of lots of tiny dots, called pixels (short for picture elements).

2) The colour of each pixel is represented by a binary code. The number of colours available in an image is related to the number of bits the code has.

3) Black-and-white images only use two colours, so they only need 1-bit to represent each pixel — 0 for white and 1 for black.

4) 2-bit images can be made up of four colours. Each pixel can be one of four binary values — 00, 01, 10 and 11.

5) You can make a greater range of shades and colours by increasing the number of bits for each pixel.

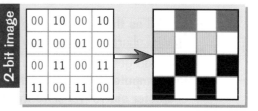

This image would have the bit pattern
0101 1010 0101 1010

Computer screens are often divided into millions of pixels arranged in rows and columns.

Increasing Colour Depth and Resolution increases the File Size

1) The colour depth is the number of bits used for each pixel.

2) Given the colour depth you can work out how many colours can be made using this formula:

Total number of colours = 2^n (where n = number of bits per pixel, or bpp)

| 1-bit image: 2^1 = 2 colours | 4-bit image: 2^4 = 16 colours | 24-bit image: 2^{24} = 16 777 216 colours |

3) Most devices use a 24-bit colour depth, with 8 bits used to indicate the levels of red, green and blue needed for each pixel. It's estimated that the human eye can see around 10 million different colours, so a 24-bit colour depth should cover every colour that you could possibly see.

4) The image resolution is the number of pixels in the image. It's sometimes given as width × height. The higher the resolution, the more pixels the image is made of, so the better the quality of the image. E.g. if an image has a resolution of 1200 × 800, it means that it is made up of 960 000 pixels. If we decreased the resolution to 600 × 400, it would only have 240 000 pixels, so a lower quality.

5) To work out how many bits an image will take up, use the formula:

File size (in bits) = image resolution x colour depth = width × height × colour depth

6) Using a greater image resolution or colour depth means that there are more bits in the image. This can give a higher-quality image, but also increases the file size.

EXAMPLE: Calculate the file size, in MB, of an 8-bit image that is 2000 pixels wide and 1000 pixels high.
1) First, use the formula to find the size in bits: 2000 × 1000 × 8 = 16 000 000 bits
2) Divide by 8 to convert to bytes: 16 000 000 ÷ 8 = 2 000 000 bytes
3) Finally, divide by 1000 twice to convert to MB: 2 000 000 ÷ 1000 ÷ 1000 = 2 MB

My friends row about image sizes — I hope there's a resolution...

Bet you didn't know images had so much going on. Remember that these types of images are called bitmaps — they're the ones made out of pixels. There is also another type called a vector image — vectors are made of simple shapes, all different blocks of colour. We tend to use them for computer-made graphics, like this picture of a distinguished goat that's wandered onto this tip.

Storing Sound

Like images, sound is made up of bits and stored in files on a computer. Or rather, digital sound is — the other type of sound, analogue, doesn't get on well with computers very much, so we've got to turn it into digital first.

Sound is Sampled and stored Digitally

1) Sound is recorded by a microphone as an <u>analogue</u> signal. Analogue signals are pieces of <u>continually changing</u> data.

2) Analogue signals need to be converted into <u>digital</u> data so that computers can read and store sound files. This is done by <u>analogue to digital converters</u>, which are found in most modern recording devices.

3) The process of converting analogue to digital is called <u>sampling</u>:

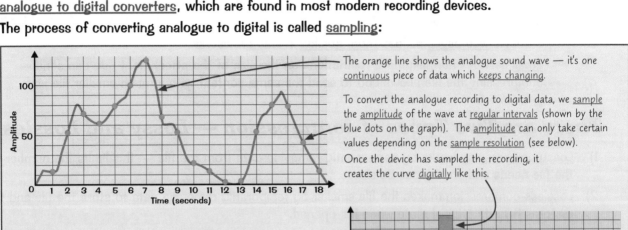

The orange line shows the analogue sound wave — it's one <u>continuous</u> piece of data which <u>keeps changing</u>.

To convert the analogue recording to digital data, we <u>sample</u> the <u>amplitude</u> of the wave at <u>regular intervals</u> (shown by the blue dots on the graph). The <u>amplitude</u> can only take certain values depending on the <u>sample resolution</u> (see below). Once the device has sampled the recording, it creates the curve <u>digitally</u> like this.

Each block of data matches where each sample was taken.

The digital data is about the same shape as the analogue wave, but it's <u>not continuous</u>. It's <u>lost</u> a lot of data — e.g. the last peak in the analogue wave is much flatter in the digital data.

The digital data can be improved by taking samples <u>more regularly</u> — most music isn't sampled every second but every couple of <u>milliseconds</u>.

Several factors affect the Size and Quality of Sound Files

1) <u>Sample rate</u> (or <u>sampling frequency</u>) is how many samples you take in a second — it's usually measured in hertz (Hz) or kilohertz (kHz). E.g. a common sample rate is 44 100 samples per second (44 100 Hz or 44.1 kHz).

2) <u>Sample resolution</u> is the number of bits available for each sample.

Sample rate × sample resolution is often called the <u>bit rate</u>.

3) You can calculate the <u>size</u> of a sound file using this <u>formula</u>:

> **File size (in bits) = Sample rate (in Hz) x sample resolution x length (in seconds)**

5) For example, if you were to sample <u>30 seconds</u> of audio with a sample resolution of <u>8 bits</u> and a sample rate of <u>500 Hz</u>, your file would be 500 x 8 x 30 = 120 000 bits.

6) <u>Increasing</u> the sample rate means the analogue recording is sampled more often. The sampled sound will be <u>better quality</u> and will more <u>closely match</u> the original recording.

7) <u>Increasing</u> the sample resolution means the digital file picks up <u>quieter sounds</u>, even if they're happening at the same time as louder ones. This will also result in a sampled sound that is closer to the <u>quality</u> of the original recording.

8) However, increasing the sample rate or sample resolution will <u>increase the file size</u>.

Anna Log talks continuously, while Digit Al just speaks in bits...

Don't mix up sample resolution with image resolution from the previous page. Really, sample resolution is the sound equivalent of colour depth — it's the number of bits used for each 'piece' of data in the file.

Compression

In the modern world, we're practically swimming in badly lit photos and subpar pop songs — so many, in fact, that you'd start to wonder how we can possibly store them all. The answer is down to data compression.

Sometimes we need to Compress files

1) Data compression is when we make file sizes smaller, while trying to make the compressed file as true to the original as possible.

2) Compressing data files has many uses:

- Smaller files take up less storage space on a device.
- Streaming and downloading files from the Internet is quicker as they take up less bandwidth.
- It allows web pages to load more quickly in web browsers.
- Email services normally have restrictions on the size of the attachment you can send — compressing the file allows you to send the same content with a much smaller file size.

There are Two Types of compression — Lossy and Lossless

1) Lossy compression works by permanently removing data from the file — this limits the number of bits the file needs and so reduces its size.

2) Lossless compression makes the file smaller by temporarily removing data to store the file and then restores it to its original state when it's opened.

	Pros	Cons	E.g. of File Types
Lossy	• Greatly reduced file size, meaning more files can be stored. • Lossy files take up less bandwidth so can be downloaded and streamed more quickly. • Commonly used — lots of software can read lossy files.	• Lossy compression loses data — the file can't be turned back into the original. • Lossy compression can't be used on text or software files as these files need to retain all the information of the original. • Lossy files are worse quality than the original. But, this loss in quality is normally unnoticeable.	• MP3 (audio) • AAC (audio) • JPEG (image)
Lossless	• Data is only removed temporarily so there is no reduction in quality — the compressed file should look or sound like the original. • Lossless files can be decompressed — turned back into the original. • Lossless compression can be used on text and software files.	• Only a slight reduction in file size, so lossless files still take up quite a bit of space on your device. E.g. a lossless song may have a file size of around 30 MB, while the same song with lossy compression may be 5 MB.	• FLAC (audio) • TIFF (image) • PNG (image)

 EXAMPLE: Phil has just heard a new band on the radio. He wants to download fifty of their songs from the Internet and store them on his smartphone to take on holiday. State which type of compression would be most appropriate in this situation and explain why.

Lossy compression would be the most appropriate. Lossy files are smaller so they would take up less bandwidth, meaning Phil could download the songs more quickly. Their smaller file size would also allow him to store them all on his smartphone without taking up too much storage space.

The best compression type? I'm afraid I'm at a loss...

Lossy files aren't as high quality as the originals, but the difference is normally unnoticeable to us unperceptive humans. This helps to explain why lossy file formats like JPEG (for photos) and MP3 (for music) are so popular — they save a lot of storage space and their inferior quality is hardly noticeable.

Run-Length Encoding

So compression is important when saving and transmitting data — but the real question is, how do you do it? Run-Length Encoding (RLE) is one of the two compression techniques that you should know (just run with it...)

Run-Length Encoding looks for Repeating Data

1) Run-Length Encoding (or RLE for short) is a form of lossless compression (see previous page). This means that the process reduces a file's size without losing any data.

2) It looks for consecutive repeating data in a file — called a run. Instead of storing each piece of repeated data separately, it just stores the number of times it repeats, and one copy of the data.

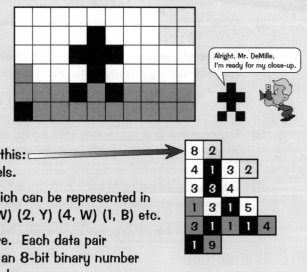

- Take a look at the bitmap image on the right.

- If the image used an 8-bit colour depth then, using the formula on p40, it would be made up of $8 \times 10 \times 6 = \underline{480 \text{ bits}}$. This can be reduced by using RLE.

- First, count the number of times the same data is repeated in each run, and store this instead.

- So this image could be compressed to look like this: E.g. the top row has 8 white, then 2 yellow pixels.

- You can store this information as data pairs, which can be represented in the format (number of pixels, colour), e.g. (8, W) (2, Y) (4, W) (1, B) etc.

- In this example, we'd have 20 data pairs to store. Each data pair consists of a number, which could be stored as an 8-bit binary number (see p34), and an 8-bit colour — so 16 bits total.

- The final compressed image would be $20 \times 16 = \underline{320 \text{ bits}}$, rather than the 480 bits that we started with — that's a 33% decrease in file size.

3) Run-length encoding is pretty easy to understand, but it's not perfect. If the data doesn't have many runs of repeated data, then the file size will not be significantly decreased.

You can also use RLE to compress Different Types of Data

1) Run-length encoding can also be applied to text. For example, say we have the string 'wwwwwhtttt'. In ASCII, this would use one byte for each character, so 10 bytes altogether.

2) Looking for runs, we can see that 'w' occurs 5 times, then 'h' once and then 't' four times. As data pairs, this would be: (5, w) (1, h) (4, t). So we can store this in 6 bytes rather than 10.

3) You can also use RLE to encode binary data. But be warned — because 1s and 0s just take up 1 bit each, you need very long runs of repeated data for it to actually reduce the size.

EXAMPLE: Use run-length encoding to compress the following binary code:

00000000 01111111 11111111 11000000 00000000

Count the number of bits in each run and write down the data pairs.

Nine 0s, then seventeen 1s and fourteen 0s. So the data pairs are (9, 0) (17, 1) (14, 0).

Each data pair could be 8 bits with 7 bits for the run lengths, and 1 bit for the actual data:

0001001 0   0010001 1   0001110 0
9 written in binary   17 written in binary   14 written in binary

Me on a rollercoaster: (1, W), (24, O), (1, !)...

Learning the content above will really help you understand how text, images and sound can be compressed without losing any data. Just remember that run-length encoding doesn't always reduce the size of a file — like buying new expensive trainers, you need long runs to make it worthwhile.

Huffman Coding

Another <u>lossless</u> compression technique that you'll need to know is Huffman coding. Enjoy. It's a good'un.

Huffman Coding uses the Frequency of each data value

1) Each <u>data value</u> in a <u>file</u> (e.g. a character in a text file) takes up the <u>same amount of space</u>. For example, text encoded in ASCII (see p39) uses 1 byte per character, but this is often <u>inefficient</u>.

2) <u>Huffman coding</u> gives <u>each data value</u> a <u>unique binary code</u> but the codes <u>vary in length</u>. It gives <u>shorter binary codes</u> to data values that appear <u>more frequently</u>.

EXAMPLE: Encode the string 'he sells seashells' using Huffman coding.

Character	Frequency
h	2
e	4
space	2
s	5
l	4
a	1

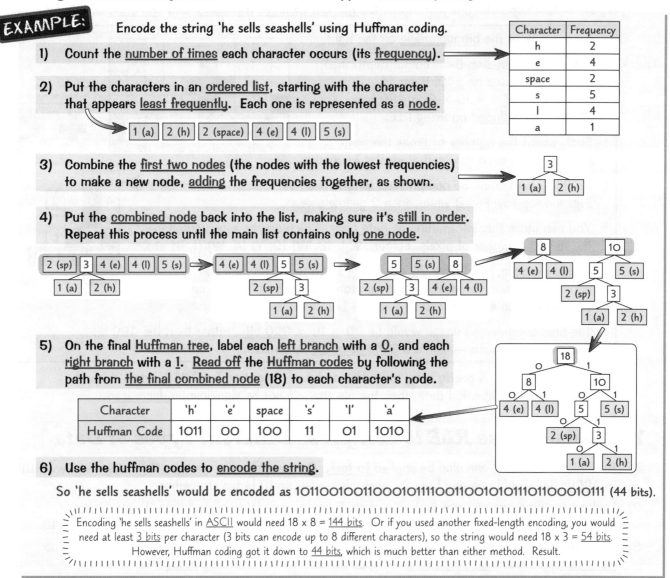

1) Count the <u>number of times</u> each character occurs (its <u>frequency</u>).

2) Put the characters in an <u>ordered list</u>, starting with the character that appears <u>least frequently</u>. Each one is represented as a <u>node</u>.

   1 (a) 2 (h) 2 (space) 4 (e) 4 (l) 5 (s)

3) Combine the <u>first two nodes</u> (the nodes with the lowest frequencies) to make a new node, <u>adding</u> the frequencies together, as shown.

4) Put the <u>combined node</u> back into the list, making sure it's <u>still in order</u>. Repeat this process until the main list contains only <u>one node</u>.

5) On the final <u>Huffman tree</u>, label each <u>left branch</u> with a <u>0</u>, and each <u>right branch</u> with a <u>1</u>. <u>Read off</u> the Huffman codes by following the path from <u>the final combined node</u> (18) to each character's node.

Character	'h'	'e'	space	's'	'l'	'a'
Huffman Code	1011	00	100	11	01	1010

6) Use the huffman codes to <u>encode the string</u>.

   So 'he sells seashells' would be encoded as 10110010011000101111001100101011011000010111 (44 bits).

   Encoding 'he sells seashells' in <u>ASCII</u> would need 18 × 8 = <u>144 bits</u>. Or if you used another fixed-length encoding, you would need at least <u>3 bits</u> per character (3 bits can encode up to 8 different characters), so the string would need 18 × 3 = <u>54 bits</u>. However, Huffman coding got it down to <u>44 bits</u>, which is much better than either method. Result.

You can also <u>decode</u> data, using either the <u>Huffman tree</u> or a <u>table of Huffman codes</u>.

EXAMPLE: Decode this binary string, using the Huffman code in the table above:
   111011000101111001011101011110100100000000111

1) Starting on the left, find the <u>first code</u> — 1 isn't a code, but <u>11</u> is the code for '<u>s</u>'. <u>Draw a line</u> after 11, and write an '<u>s</u>'.

   11|1011|00|01|01|11|100|1011|1010|11|1101|00|100|00|00|01|11
   s   h   e l l s   h   a   s l   e   e l s

2) Keep going until it's <u>completely decoded</u>. So the decoded string is shells hassle eels.

Don't go off in a huff man, it's only a type of compression...

Huffman coding is a really handy compression technique — plus, Huffman trees look particularly splendid in Autumn. You should know how to both encode and decode data using a Huffman tree.

Revision Questions for Section Four

Section Four is done and dusted, so all you've got to do now is try these questions, then put your feet up.

- Try these questions and <u>tick off each one</u> when you <u>get it right</u>.
- When you've done <u>all the questions</u> for a topic and are <u>completely happy</u> with it, tick off the topic.

Logic and Units (p31-33) ☐

1) For each of the 3 main logic gates:
   a) Draw its symbol.
   b) State how many inputs and outputs it has.
   c) Draw its truth table.

2)* Draw the truth table for the logic diagram on the right.

3) Why is binary used by computers?

4) Put these units in order of size: Terabyte, Byte, Kilobyte, Gigabyte, Megabyte

5)* A hard drive has a storage capacity of 200 megabytes.
   a) How many gigabytes is this?
   b) How many bits is this?

Binary and Hexadecimal (p34-38) ☑

6)* Add the binary numbers 01011101 and 00110010.

7) What effect do left and right shifts have on binary numbers?

8)* Convert the following decimal numbers to:
   a) binary
   b) hexadecimal
   (i) 17
   (ii) 148
   (iii) 240

9)* Convert the following binary numbers to:
   a) decimal
   b) hexadecimal
   (i) 00111000
   (ii) 10011111
   (iii) 101011

10)* Convert these hexadecimal numbers to:
   a) decimal
   b) binary
   (i) 4A
   (ii) 75
   (iii) BD9

11) Give three reasons why programmers prefer hexadecimal over binary and decimal.

Characters, Images and Sound (p39-41) ☐

12) What is the definition of a character set?

13) Give the four types of characters that are included in a character set.

14) What are the two main character sets? Give a feature of each.

15) Define the following terms: a) pixel   b) bitmap   c) colour depth   d) image resolution

16) Give two effects of choosing a greater image resolution or colour depth for an image.

17) In no more than four bullet points, explain how audio sampling works.

18) Give a definition for each of the following and explain what happens when you increase each of them:
   a) sample rate   b) sample resolution

Compression and Coding (p42-44) ☑

19) Give four reasons why you might want to compress data.

20) What is the difference between lossy compression and lossless compression?

21) Give three reasons why you might want to use: a) lossy compression   b) lossless compression

22)* The file letters.txt contains the string 'PPPPQQRRRSSSSSSSPPPPPQQQ'.
   a) Encode this string using run-length encoding.
   b) Draw a Huffman tree for this string.
   c) Calculate the number of bits needed to store the string if it was encoded with:
     (i) ASCII   (ii) Huffman coding   (iii) Run-length encoding (if each data pair used 2 bytes).

*Answers on p73

Computer Systems

Now it's time to take a step back and ask yourself the most important question — what even is a computer?

A Computer is a Machine that Processes Data

1) The purpose of a computer is to take <u>data</u>, <u>process</u> it, then <u>output</u> it.
Computers were created to help process data and complete tasks <u>more efficiently</u> than humans.

2) A <u>computer system</u> consists of <u>hardware</u> and <u>software</u> that work together to process data / complete tasks.

> - Hardware is the <u>physical</u> stuff that makes up your computer system, like the CPU, motherboard, monitor and printer.
> - Software is the <u>programs</u> that a computer system runs. You can have <u>application software</u> (programs that help the user perform specific tasks, e.g. word processors, web browsers, email clients, games, etc.) and <u>system software</u> (operating systems, utilities, etc. — see p53-55).

> *External pieces of hardware like the keyboard, mouse and printer are called <u>peripherals</u>.*

3) There are <u>many types</u> of computer system. These range from small devices like calculators and watches, up to large <u>supercomputers</u> used by banks or for scientific applications. Computers may be <u>general purpose</u> (designed to perform <u>many tasks</u>, e.g. PCs and tablets) or <u>dedicated systems</u> (designed for <u>one particular</u> function, e.g. controlling traffic lights or an aeroplane).

Embedded Systems are Computers inside a Larger System

1) <u>Embedded systems</u> are computers <u>built into other devices</u>, like dishwashers, microwaves and TVs. They are usually dedicated systems.

2) Embedded systems are often used as <u>control systems</u> — they <u>monitor</u> and <u>control</u> machinery in order to achieve a desired result. E.g. In a <u>dishwasher</u> the embedded system could control the water pumps and water release mechanisms, manage the various dishwasher cycles and control the thermostat to keep the water at an appropriate temperature.

3) As they're <u>dedicated</u> to a single task, embedded systems are usually easier to <u>design</u>, cheaper to <u>produce</u>, and more <u>efficient</u> at doing their task than a general purpose computer.

Computers contain Components which Work Together

This section is all about the main hardware components of a computer.
As a <u>genuinely fun</u> warm-up, let's take a look inside a typical desktop PC.

<u>Power supply</u> — supplies power to motherboard, optical and hard drives, and other hardware.

<u>Case cooling fan</u> — extracts hot air from the computer case.

<u>CPU heat sink and cooling fan</u> — keeps the CPU at a steady temperature (CPUs generate a lot of heat).

<u>CPU</u> (hidden under the heat sink) — the most important component. Does all the processing. See p47-48.

The <u>graphics card</u> slots in here. See p50.

<u>Optical drive</u> — for read/writing of optical discs. See p52.

<u>Ghost</u> in the machine.

<u>RAM sticks</u> (computer memory) slot in here. See p49-50.

<u>Hard Disk Drive</u> — Internal secondary storage. See p51.

<u>Motherboard</u> — The main circuit board in the computer, where the hardware is connected.

Hardware — clothes that make you look dead tough, innit...

Make sure you know all of these components before moving on — they'll crop up a lot in this section...

The CPU

The CPU is mega-important — it's the main component of a computer, so here are two whole pages about it. Yay.

The CPU is the Central Processing Unit

1) The CPU is the brain of the computer system.
2) It processes all of the data and instructions that make the system work.
3) The processing power of a CPU depends on different characteristics, like its clock speed, number of cores and cache size and type — see p50.
4) The CPU architecture describes the main components of the CPU, how they interact with each other, and with other parts of the computer system. Von Neumann and Harvard are the two main types of architecture. You will need to know about Von Neumann — see next page.

CPUs contain 1000s of gold pins — some of these transmit data, others supply power to the CPU. (Aside: CPUs are shiny and pretty)

The CPU has Five Main Parts

The Control Unit (CU)

- The control unit is in overall control of the CPU. Its main job is to execute program instructions by following the fetch-decode-execute cycle (see next page).
- It controls the flow of data inside the CPU (to registers, ALU, cache — see below) and outside the CPU (to main memory and input/output devices).

The Arithmetic Logic Unit (ALU)

- The ALU basically does all the calculations.
- It completes simple addition and subtraction, compares the size of numbers and can do multiplications and divisions using repeated addition and subtraction.
- It performs logic operations such as AND, OR and NOT (p31) and binary shifts (p36) — remember, computers process binary data.
- Registers (see below) are used to store intermediate results of calculations.

> 3 PLUS 2 IS 5!
> TRUE OR FALSE IS TRUE!

The Cache

- The cache is very fast memory in the CPU. It's slower than the registers (see below), but faster than RAM (p49).
- It stores regularly used data so that the CPU can access it quickly the next time it's needed. When the CPU requests data, it checks the cache first to see if the data is there. If not, it will fetch it from RAM.
- Caches have a very low capacity and are expensive compared to RAM and secondary storage.

The Clock

- The clock sends out a signal that continually cycles between 1 and 0, usually at a constant rate.
- The signal is used to synchronise when instructions will be carried out (like a metronome).
- The number of clock cycles (or clock ticks) per second is called the clock speed (p50).

Buses

- Buses are collections of wires that are used to transmit data between components of the CPU, and to other parts of the computer system.
- A processor may have separate buses for carrying data, instructions and memory addresses.

The CPU also contains various registers which temporarily hold tiny bits of data needed by the CPU. They are super-quick to read/write to, way quicker than any other form of memory.

What's a CPU's favourite outdoor activity? Geocaching...

It's important that you know all about the different components of a CPU. Try learning everything you can about each one, then cover up the page and write down as many notes as you can.

The CPU

Now let's look at the Von Neumann architecture and what the CPU does in a bit more detail.
Von Neumann came up with his design in 1945 and it still describes how most computers work today.

Von Neumann's Design Revolutionised Computing

The Von Neumann architecture describes a system where the CPU runs <u>programs</u> stored in <u>memory</u>.
Programs consist of <u>instructions</u> and <u>data</u> which are stored in memory <u>addresses</u>.

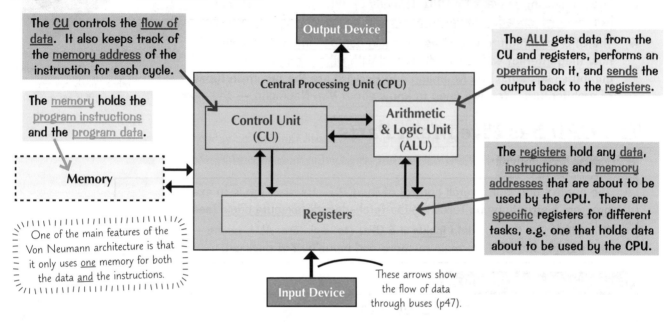

The <u>CU</u> controls the <u>flow of data</u>. It also keeps track of the <u>memory address</u> of the instruction for each cycle.

The <u>memory</u> holds the <u>program instructions</u> and the <u>program data</u>.

One of the main features of the Von Neumann architecture is that it only uses <u>one</u> memory for both the data <u>and</u> the instructions.

The <u>ALU</u> gets data from the CU and registers, performs an <u>operation</u> on it, and <u>sends</u> the output back to the <u>registers</u>.

The <u>registers</u> hold any <u>data</u>, <u>instructions</u> and <u>memory addresses</u> that are about to be used by the CPU. There are <u>specific</u> registers for different tasks, e.g. one that holds data about to be used by the CPU.

These arrows show the flow of data through buses (p47).

CPUs follow the Fetch-Decode-Execute Cycle

Essentially, <u>all a CPU does</u> is carry out instructions, one after another, billions of times a second. The <u>Fetch-Decode-Execute</u> cycle describes how it does it.

Each Fetch-Decode-Execute cycle will take multiple clock cycles (see previous page).

FETCH INSTRUCTION

1) The <u>control unit</u> reads the <u>memory address</u> of the next CPU instruction.
2) The <u>instruction</u> stored in that address is copied from <u>memory</u> to one of the <u>registers</u>.
3) The memory address in the <u>control unit</u> is <u>incremented</u> to point to the address of the <u>next</u> instruction, ready for the <u>next cycle</u>.

EXECUTE INSTRUCTION

The instruction is <u>performed</u>. This could be: <u>load data</u> from memory, <u>write data</u> to memory, do a <u>calculation</u> or <u>logic</u> operation (using the ALU), change the address in the <u>CU</u>, or <u>halt</u> the program.

DECODE INSTRUCTION

1) The instruction that was copied from memory is <u>decoded</u> by the control unit.
2) The control unit <u>prepares</u> for the next step, e.g. by loading other values into the registers.

Well, now I know why my computer goes through so many dogs...

I won't lie to you, this page is tougher than a really tough piece of toffee. Just keep going through the cycle until it sticks — it uses the memory address to fetch the instruction, it decodes the instruction and gets everything ready for execution, and then it actually carries the instruction out. The parts of the CPU are important as well — remember, the ALU does the calculations, the registers hold data and instructions waiting to be used, and the CU tells everything else what to do.

Memory

As you'll have gathered from the last page, memory is a pretty fundamental part of a computer. It contains all the instructions that the CPU follows. Without memory, a computer wouldn't know what to do with itself.

RAM is High Speed, Volatile memory

1) RAM (or Random Access Memory) is used as the main memory in a computer. It can be read and written to. RAM is volatile.

   - Volatile memory is temporary memory. It requires power to retain its data.
   - Non-volatile memory is permanent memory — it keeps its contents even when it has no power.

2) The main memory is where all data, files and programs are stored while they're being used.

3) When a computer boots up, the operating system is copied from secondary storage to RAM.

4) When software applications, documents and files are opened, they are copied from secondary storage to RAM. They stay in RAM until the files or applications are closed.

5) RAM is slower than the CPU cache, but way faster than secondary storage.

Secondary storage is covered on p51-52.

That's RAM covered, which can mean only ROM thing...

ROM tells the CPU how to Boot Up

1) ROM ('Read Only Memory') is non-volatile memory. As it says on the tin, it can only be read, not written to.

2) ROM comes on a small, factory-made chip built into the motherboard.

3) It contains all the instructions a computer needs to properly boot up. These instructions are called the BIOS (Basic Input Output System).

The BIOS is a type of firmware — hardware-specific software built in to a device. Embedded systems (p46) are controlled by firmware.

4) As soon as the computer is powered on, the CPU reads the instructions from ROM. This tells the CPU to perform self checks and set up the computer, e.g. test the memory is working OK, see what hardware is present and copy the operating system into RAM.

5) Although the CPU can only read ROM, it is possible to update ('flash') the BIOS on a ROM chip.

> ROM chips often use flash memory. This is a very common type of non-volatile memory that stores data in electrical circuits by trapping electrons. It's used in SD cards, USB sticks and solid state drives (SSDs). There's loads about flash devices on p51.

Systems have Different RAM/ROM Requirements

The amount of RAM and ROM that a system needs depends on the purpose and type of the system.

Non-embedded systems

- Non-embedded systems usually have much more RAM than ROM because they often need to write data to main memory.
- ROM is typically only used for BIOS, which doesn't require much memory.
- ROM and RAM are usually stored on the motherboard, away from the CPU.

Embedded systems

- Embedded systems usually have more ROM than RAM because they don't write much (if any) data to memory.
- They don't tend to have secondary storage (p51-52) so ROM is used to store all programs.
- ROM and RAM are often stored on the same chip as the CPU to reduce physical space needed and cost.

Woah, woah, back off — this memory's volatile...

The memory (RAM) is where the computer puts everything it's working on. It's really, really, super important that you don't confuse memory with secondary storage. So if a computer has a 2 TB (see p33) hard drive, never say it has 2 TB of memory. Don't even think about it — it'd just be plain wrong.

CPU and System Performance

All sorts of things affect the speed of a computer system, but the biggest factors are usually to do with the hardware. Choice of CPU, RAM and GPU (see below) can all have big effects on performance.

CPU Performance depends on Clock Speed, Cores and Cache

Clock speed

- For most desktop computers, clock speed (see p47) is somewhere around 3.5 GHz (i.e. 3.5 billion clock cycles per second). This determines the number of instructions a single processor core can carry out per second — the higher the clock speed, the more instructions that can be carried out per second.
- Some CPUs can be overclocked to make them run at a higher clock speed than the factory-set rate. But it's risky if not done properly — it can make CPUs overheat, causing crashes or permanent damage to the system. High performance cooling systems (e.g. water cooling) are usually needed.

CPU Cores

- Each core in a CPU can process data independently of the rest.
- The more cores a CPU has, the more instructions it can carry out at once, so the faster it can process a batch of data.
- Most PCs and smartphones have 4 or more cores these days.

It's not quite as simple as 'doubling the number of cores doubles performance'. Software needs to be designed to use multicore processing. And not all processing tasks can be split evenly between cores — some steps will depend on others, meaning one core may end up waiting for another core to catch up.

Cache Size

- The cache (p47) is data storage inside the CPU that's much faster than RAM.
- A larger CPU cache gives the CPU faster access to more data it needs to process.

Cache Type

- There are different levels of cache memory — L1, L2 and L3. The higher the level, the more it can hold, but the slower it is.
- Cache speed is based on how far it is from the CPU. L1 is quick because it's on the CPU itself, while L3 is often on the motherboard so it's slower.

Generally, CPUs with higher clock speeds, more cores or larger caches of lower levels will have better performance, but will also be more expensive.

Overall Performance is affected by Other Components too

RAM
1) If a computer has too little RAM, it may not be able to keep all application data loaded at once, slowing the system down.
2) The more RAM, the more applications or more memory-intensive applications it can smoothly run, making it faster overall.
3) If the computer already has plenty of RAM to run everything the user wants, increasing RAM may make no difference to performance.

RAM comes on sticks which plug into slots on the motherboard.

GPU
1) GPUs (graphics processing units) handle graphics and image processing. They relieve the processing load on the CPU, freeing it to do other things.
2) Computers have basic GPUs integrated onto the motherboard or the CPU, but you can install a dedicated GPU (graphics card) to improve performance in graphics-intensive applications, e.g. PC gaming and design software.

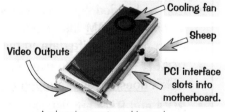

Cooling fan

Sheep

Video Outputs

PCI interface slots into motherboard.

A whopping-great graphics card — explains why gaming PCs are massive.

You can buy apples with 4 cores now? Don't be daft...

To be honest, there are quite a few simplifications going on here. In the real world, there's a lot more to CPU performance than cores, cache and clock speed. But this level of detail is all you need at GCSE. Using SSDs rather than traditional hard drives is another way to speed up a computer — see p51.

Secondary Storage

"Secondary storage!", I hear you cry. "But what about primary?" It's OK, we've just covered that, as you'll see...

There are Two Main Tiers of Storage

1) Primary storage refers to the memory areas that the CPU can access directly, like CPU registers, cache, ROM and RAM. Primary storage has the fastest read/write speeds and is mostly volatile (p49).

2) Secondary storage is non-volatile storage that isn't directly accessible by the CPU. It's where all data (applications, user files and the OS) are stored when not in use. It includes magnetic hard disk drives, solid state drives, CDs and SD cards. Read/write speeds for secondary storage are much slower compared to primary storage.

There's also tertiary storage, which is used for long term data storage (mainly used for archives and backups of huge amounts of data).

Magnetic Hard Disks are High-Capacity, Reliable Storage

1) Hard disk drives (HDDs) are the traditional internal storage in PCs and laptops.

2) A hard disk drive is made up of a stack of magnetised metal disks spinning at a rate between 5400 and 15000 rpm (revolutions per minute).

3) Data is stored magnetically in small areas called sectors within circular tracks. Read/write heads on a moving arm are used to access sectors on the disks.

4) Portable HDDs are popular for backing up and transporting large amounts of data.

5) Despite their moving parts, HDDs are generally very long lasting and reliable, although they could be damaged by large impacts like being dropped.

Data track
Sector
Read / Write head
Movable arm

Other types of magnetic storage

- Another type of magnetic storage is magnetic tape. It has a very high capacity and an extremely low cost per GB. It's often used by large organisations for backing up large amounts of data.

- Reels of tape are stored in plastic cassettes. Tapes are read/written sequentially by the tape drive i.e. from beginning to end. This means it can be slow when finding specific data stored on them, but once it's in the right place, reading/writing to the tape is very fast.

Solid State Drives are Fast and Reliable Secondary Storage

1) Solid State Drives (SSDs) are storage devices with no moving parts. Most of them use a type of flash memory (see p49). SSDs are used for the same purpose as HDDs — for internal storage.

2) SSDs have significantly faster read/write times than HDDs. Using a SSD rather than traditional HDD can give much quicker times for booting up and opening programs and files.

3) Hybrid drives exist which use solid state storage for the OS and programs, and a hard disk for data.

4) Like HDDs, portable SSDs can be used to back up and transport data.

Other types of flash storage

- USB pen drives and memory cards (e.g. SD cards) are also flash-based, solid-state storage.

- They're much slower than SSDs and have a much shorter read/write life.

- They're used to expand the storage capacity of small devices like cameras, smartphones and tablets (which are too small for SSDs or HDDs). Their capacity is very high relative to their tiny size.

HDDs vs SSDs — Who wins, You Decide...

Advantages of HDDs	Advantages of SSDs
• HDDs are cheaper.	• SSDs are faster.
• Both are high capacity, but HDDs are higher.	• SSDs don't need defragmenting (see p55).
• HDDs have a longer read/write life than SSDs — SSDs can only be written a certain number of times before they begin to deteriorate.	• SSDs are more shock-proof than HDDs.
	• HDDs make some noise, SSDs are silent.

Secondary Storage

Be careful with your terminology. Storage <u>media</u> refers to the actual thing that holds the data, e.g. optical discs (see below). A storage <u>device</u> is the thing that reads/writes data to media, e.g. HDDs or optical drive.

Optical Discs are Cheap and Robust Secondary Storage

1) Optical discs are things like <u>CDs</u>, <u>DVDs</u> and <u>Blu-Ray</u>™ discs.

2) CDs can hold around 700 MB of data, DVDs can hold around 4.7 GB and Blu-Rays can hold around 25 GB.

3) Optical discs come in three forms:

- <u>read-only</u> (e.g. CD-ROM / DVD-ROM / BD-ROM)
- <u>write-once</u> (e.g. CD-R / DVD-R / BD-R)
- <u>rewritable</u> (e.g. CD-RW / DVD-RW / BD-RW)

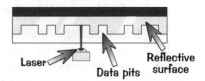

Laser   Data pits   Reflective surface

Data is stored as <u>microscopic indentations</u> on the shiny surface of the disc. Data is read by shining a laser beam on the surface and detecting changes in the position of the <u>reflected beam</u>.

4) Nowadays, their use is <u>declining</u>:
- <u>Streaming</u> and <u>download</u> services have reduced the need for optical discs.
- Modern devices like <u>phones</u> and <u>tablets</u> don't have optical drives.
- DVD-Rs and DVD-RWs used to be popular for backing up data, but they can't compete with flash storage devices due to their <u>low capacity</u> per disc, very <u>slow</u> read/write speeds and poor reliability of <u>RW</u> discs.

5) They do have some <u>advantages</u> — they're very cheap (per GB), portable, and won't be damaged by <u>water</u> or <u>shocks</u> (although they are easily <u>scratched</u>).

Optical discs are still useful as mirrors. Or, bury them in flowerbeds to scare away cats.

Cloud Storage uses the Internet to store files and applications

<u>Cloud storage</u> is a service where files can be <u>uploaded</u> via the <u>Internet</u> to a <u>remote server</u> (where it is usually stored on HDDs/SSDs). You normally pay a <u>subscription</u>, though some provide a <u>limited service</u> for <u>free</u> (p67).

Pros of the cloud
- Users can access files from <u>any connected device</u>.
- Files can be <u>shared</u> with others or made <u>public</u>.
- Easy to <u>increase</u> how much <u>storage</u> is available.
- <u>No</u> need to buy <u>expensive hardware</u> to store data.
- <u>No</u> need to pay <u>IT staff</u> to manage the hardware.
- Cloud host provides <u>security</u> and <u>backups</u> for you.
- Can be <u>cheap/free</u> if <u>not much storage</u> is required.

Cons of the cloud
- Need <u>connection to the Internet</u> to access files.
- Upload/download speed depends on <u>bandwidth</u>.
- <u>Dependent on host</u> for security and backups.
- Stored data can be <u>vulnerable</u> to hackers (p69).
- Unclear who has <u>ownership</u> over cloud data.
- Subscription fees for using cloud <u>storage</u> may be expensive in the <u>long term</u>.

A quick Summary...

It can get pretty confusing with all this 'thingy is faster than thingy which is cheaper than thingy but holds less than thingy'. So here's a summary of relative <u>speeds</u>, <u>costs</u> and <u>capacities</u>.

Optical Disc	Memory Card		Magnetic Tape	HDD		SSD
Slowest		**Average read/write speed**				*Fastest*

Magnetic Tape		Optical Disc	HDD		Memory Card	SSD
Cheapest			**Average cost (per GB)**			*Priciest*

Optical Disc	Memory Card		SSD	HDD		Magnetic Tape
Lowest			**Average capacity**			*Highest*

The speed, cost and capacity of cloud storage depends a lot on the service and on your Internet connection.

Harder, Better, Faster, Stronger... cheaper, more reliable... more shiny...

Poor old optical discs. I remember when this happened to Mr Floppy. It made me very sad... Here's Mr Floppy with his remarkable 1.44 MB of storage.

System Software — The OS

System software is software designed to run and maintain a computer system. By far the most important one is the operating system (OS). There's also utility software (p55) but that's very much the runner up.

Operating Systems manage Hardware and run Software

An Operating System (OS) is a complex piece of software found on most computer systems.
The main functions of an OS are to:

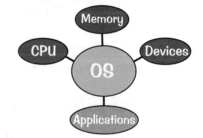

- Communicate with input and output devices via device drivers.
- Provide a platform for applications to run on, and a user interface.
- Control memory management and allocation.
- Organise the CPU and its processing tasks.
- Deal with file management and disk management.
- Manage system security and user accounts.

Let's look at each function in a bit more detail...

The OS Communicates with I/O Devices through Drivers

I/O (input/output) devices allow computers to take inputs (e.g. through a keyboard, microphone, webcam, etc.) and give outputs (e.g. through a monitor, speakers, printer, etc.). Operating systems use device drivers to communicate with I/O devices connected to the computer system:

- Every I/O device connected to the computer system requires a device driver. Drivers essentially act as a 'translator' for the signals between the OS and the device.

- When a computer is booted up, the OS will choose the correct device drivers for the device it detects. If new devices are connected to the computer, the system may automatically find and install a new, matching driver.

- Device manufacturers may release updates to device drivers in order to fix bugs, add features or improve the performance of their device. Updates may be installed automatically by the OS or manually by the user.

The OS also manages Applications

1) Operating systems provide a platform for applications to run on, and manage system resources (see next page) to allow computers to run multiple applications at once — known as multitasking.

2) It also allows applications to access hardware and other peripheral devices as needed, including access to RAM (see next page) and secondary storage (e.g. so files can be opened and saved).

3) The OS also provides a user interface that applications are accessed through. Most desktop computers traditionally use graphical interfaces (GUIs) that are WIMP-based, where applications are displayed with windows, icons, menus and pointers.

4) These interfaces are ideal for use with a mouse and keyboard, but devices with different input methods (e.g. smartphones with touchscreens) may have very different interfaces.

5) Applications are usually written for a particular OS and will take advantage of its features, e.g. using standard windows and menus in a WIMP interface, or allowing users to tap, pinch and swipe on a touchscreen device.

©iStock.com/valio84sl

You can swipe between screens or tap an icon to open it on Android™.

A driver lets a computer speak to a mouse? If you say so...

Remember, the OS is the boss of the computer system. It controls hardware via drivers, allows the computer to run applications and gives you an interface to interact with them through. So yeah, it's important. Make sure you've got your head round everything on this page before moving on.

System Software — The OS

The OS is in charge of Memory Management

1) When an application is <u>opened</u>, the OS copies the <u>necessary</u> parts of the application to <u>memory</u>, followed by <u>additional</u> parts when they are required. The OS will decide if applications or features have been used recently — if <u>not</u>, they may be <u>removed</u> from memory.

2) The OS manages <u>how much</u> RAM a program has access to. This will depend on the program — for example, <u>image editing</u> software usually uses a lot of memory, while <u>text editors</u> need much less RAM. Certain things, like having <u>more documents</u> open, can make a program require <u>additional memory</u>.

3) When running <u>multiple</u> applications at once, the OS makes sure that they <u>don't overwrite</u> or <u>interfere</u> with each other by allocating certain applications certain memory addresses, keeping their processes in separate locations.

The OS tells the CPU what to Process

System software also creates processes, which run in the background.

What time do you call this, Mr Process?

It won't happen again, Mr CPU sir.

1) When an application is <u>launched</u>, it creates one or more <u>processes</u>. Each process has instructions that it needs the CPU to execute. However, CPUs can only carry out instructions from <u>one process</u> at a time.

2) <u>Operating systems</u> deal with this by using <u>scheduling</u> to determine the <u>most efficient order</u> for the CPU to execute instructions.

3) Each process is allocated a '<u>priority</u>' by the OS. The CPU carries out the instructions from the highest-priority processes first, and the other processes <u>wait</u> in a queue.

4) The OS may interrupt the current CPU process if a higher-priority process becomes available.

5) In order to allow <u>multitasking</u>, the CPU <u>swaps between</u> different processes <u>very rapidly</u> — remember, most CPUs can carry out <u>billions</u> of instructions in a second (p50).

The OS handles File and Disk Management

1) Computers store data as <u>files</u>. Images, music, videos and spreadsheets are all just collections of data. <u>File extensions</u> (for example .jpg, .mp3, .mpeg) tell the computer which <u>software</u> should be used to open the file.

2) The OS is responsible for <u>file management</u> — the organisation of data into a usable <u>hierarchical structure</u>. It also deals with the <u>movement</u>, <u>editing</u> and <u>deletion</u> of data.

3) The OS manages the <u>hard disk</u>. It splits the <u>physical disk</u> into storage <u>sectors</u>, decides which sectors to <u>write data</u> to, and keeps track of <u>free space</u> on the disk. Ideally, the data for a <u>single</u> file would be placed in <u>adjacent</u> sectors, but this isn't always possible (p55).

Utilities like <u>File Explorer</u> allow users to <u>navigate</u> and <u>edit</u> the file structure or access their files.

4) The OS also organises and maintains the hard disk with <u>utility software</u> (see p55) like <u>defragmentation software</u>.

Operating Systems manage System Security

1) Most popular OSs include ways of keeping data stored on a system <u>secure</u>. One common way in which they do this is through <u>user account control</u>. User accounts allow different users to be <u>granted</u> or <u>denied access</u> to specific data or resources on a computer system.

2) On most desktop operating systems, each user has access to <u>their own personal data</u> and <u>desktop</u>, but cannot access other users' personal data, unless they are a <u>system administrator</u>.

3) Operating systems may have <u>anti-theft measures</u> to prevent other users from accessing locked devices or accounts to steal information. User accounts may be <u>password</u>, or <u>pin</u> protected. Some devices also require a user to draw a specific <u>pattern</u> on the screen, or have <u>fingerprint</u> or <u>retina</u> scanners.

Now, if only my OS could manage my washing up for me too...

If you didn't believe me before that the OS is incredibly important, I bet you do now. Once you're done learning this page, go say thank you to your OS for everything it does for you. It deserves some love.

System Software — Utilities

Operating systems are amazing things, but they'd be less amazing without the tools of their trade — utilities.

Utility Software helps to Maintain a computer

Utility system software refers to any software used to maintain or configure a computer. Many useful utilities are installed with the operating system, but you can install other ones to perform additional tasks.

Defragmentation

Files are stored on a hard disk in available spaces. Ideally, whole files would be stored together, but as files are moved and deleted, gaps appear on the disk. The OS has to split new files up to fill the gaps. This makes reading these files slower as the read/write head has to move back and forth across the disk. Defragmentation puts the files back into one block and collects the free space together:

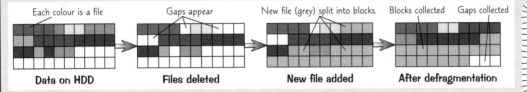

Each colour is a file — Data on HDD

Gaps appear — Files deleted

New file (grey) split into blocks. — New file added

Blocks collected   Gaps collected — After defragmentation

As SSDs have no moving parts, fragmentation doesn't slow them down — in fact, defragmenting them can actually shorten their lifespan.

Disk Health

Over time, hard drives can start to deteriorate, causing corrupted data and slow read/write speeds. Disk health utilities scan the drive for problems and fix issues where possible.

Compression

Compression software reduces the size of files so they take up less disk space (see p42). It's used loads on the Internet to make files quicker to download. Standard file formats include .zip and .rar. Compressed files need to be extracted before they can be used.

Encryption

Encryption software (see p64) scrambles (encrypts) data to stop third-parties from accessing it. Encrypted data can be decrypted using a special 'key'.

Backup

A backup is a copy of a computer system's files and settings stored externally that can be restored in the event of data loss. Data loss can happen for many reasons — fire, theft, flood, malware, hardware failure, or 'oops I accidentally selected all and pressed delete'. A backup utility is software with facilities such as scheduling of regular backups, creating rescue disks, disk images, and options for how much data to backup.

Cause of data loss #433

Virus Scanners

These inspect each file on your computer, looking for viruses. They usually have a list of known viruses to check for — they need to be updated regularly so they don't miss anything.

System Cleanup

Programs like web browsers leave a lot of temporary files on your hard drive, which can end up taking up lots of space unnecessarily. System cleanup utilities go through and get rid of files like these.

Utility software — exactly what it says on the tin...

Remember, utilities are bits of software that help maintain your system. There are plenty more you could mention in the exam, e.g. system restore, file managers, antispyware, firewalls, software auto-update, etc.

Revision Questions for Section Five

Well, that wraps up Section 5. You should be an expert on computer systems now, but we'd better just check:
- Try these questions and tick off each one when you get it right.
- When you've done all the questions for a topic and are completely happy with it, tick off the topic.

Computer Systems and the CPU (p46-48) ☑

1) First things first, what is a computer?
2) Define hardware and software.
3) Give one example of system software and one example of application software.
4) What's an embedded system?
5) What's a control system?
6) Explain the role of the control unit in the CPU.
7) What does ALU stand for and what does it do?
8) What is cache and what is it used for?
9) Describe the function of the clock.
10) What's a bus? (And I don't mean the 151 to Worcester Park...)
11) Sketch a Von Neumann computer.
12) Describe what happens at each stage of the CPU fetch-decode-execute cycle.

Memory and Computer Performance (p49-50) ☑

13) What's the difference between volatile and non-volatile memory?
14) What does RAM stand for? Describe how RAM is used in a computer system.
15) Could changing the amount of RAM affect the performance of the computer? Give reasons for your answer.
16) Explain why ROM is required by a computer system.
17) Which usually has more RAM: an embedded system or a non-embedded system?
18) Name three characteristics of a processor that may affect its performance.

Secondary Storage (p51-52) ☑

19) Define primary and secondary storage and give an example of each.
20) Who would win in a fight between an HDD and SSD? Give a blow by blow commentary of the match.
21) Why might someone choose magnetic tape as a form of storage?
22) List four uses of flash memory.
23) What are the pros and cons of:
    a) optical discs?   b) cloud storage?
24) Draw a diagram to summarise cost, speed and capacity for different types of secondary storage.

System Software (p53-55) ☑

25) List six functions of an operating system.
26) Explain how device drivers are used in a computer system.
27) Describe how the OS manages:
    a) applications   b) memory   c) the CPU   d) files and disk space
28) Give three ways in which an OS might keep your files secure.
29) List seven types of utility software and explain what they do.

Networks

When you connect a device to another one, you're creating a network — networks allow devices to share information and resources. Here we'll look at the types of network you'll need to know for your exam.

A LAN is a Local Area Network

1) A LAN covers a small geographical area located on a single site.
2) All the hardware for a LAN is owned by the organisation that uses it.
3) LANs can be wired (e.g. with Ethernet cables) or wireless — see next page.
4) You'll often find LANs in businesses, schools and universities.
5) Lots of homes have a LAN to connect various devices, such as PCs, tablets, smart TVs and printers.

A WAN is a network that Connects LANs

1) WAN stands for Wide Area Network. A WAN connects LANs that are in different geographical locations. For example, a business with offices in three different countries would need a WAN for all their devices to connect together.
2) Unlike a LAN, organisations hire infrastructure (e.g. communication lines) from telecommunications companies, who own and manage the WAN. This is because a WAN is much more expensive to set up than a LAN.
3) WANs may be connected using telephone lines (copper or fibre optic), satellite links or radio links.
4) The Internet is, of course, the biggest WAN (and in my opinion, the best).

A PAN is a Personal Network

1) Personal Area Networks (PANs) connect devices over a very short range. They're normally centred around a single user, and are often used to transmit between mobile/wearable devices (e.g. smartphones, smartwatches, headphones, etc.).
2) PANs often use common wireless technology (e.g. Bluetooth®) to connect devices. A Bluetooth® signal is quite strong, but has a very short range which makes it ideal for connecting devices in the same room.
3) PANs are handy as they usually don't require any additional hardware, just the devices themselves. This also means you can create a PAN on the move.

Networking Computers has Benefits and Drawbacks

BENEFITS

1) Sharing files is easier — network users can access the same files, work on them at the same time and copy files between machines.
2) You can share the same hardware (like printers) between multiple devices.
3) You can install and update software on all computers at once, rather than one-by-one.
4) You can communicate across a network cheaply and easily, e.g. with email.
5) User accounts can be stored centrally, so users can log in from any device on the network.

DRAWBACKS

1) They can be expensive to set up, as you often need a lot of extra hardware (see next page).
2) Networks can be vulnerable to hacking (see p69), and malware (p62) can easily spread between networked computers.
3) Some networks are dependent on one or more servers (see p59). If those servers go down it can be very disruptive for people trying to use the network.
4) Large networks are difficult to manage and may require employing a specialist to maintain them.

Don't LANguish at the bottom of the class — learn this page...

Right then. Make sure you're absolutely clear about the differences between the three types of network before moving on. Remember, companies use their own cables for LANs, but they hire lines for WANs. And if you forget about PANs, the PANstrosity will find you and sink its grisly blue tooth into you...

Networks — Wired and Wireless

Connecting devices doesn't magically happen. To create a network, you usually need certain pieces of hardware...

Networks require lots of Hardware

1) A Network Interface Card (NIC) is a piece of hardware inside a device that allows it to connect to networks. NICs exist for both wired and wireless connections.

2) Switches are used to connect devices on a LAN, while routers transmit data between different networks, and are most commonly used to connect to the Internet. Most home 'routers' are in fact a router, switch and WAP (see below) all-in-one.

3) Wired networks can use different cables to connect devices — the choice of cable usually depends on cost, bandwidth and how far you want to transmit data.

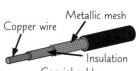
Bandwidth is the amount of data that can be sent across a network in a given time.

- Fibre optic cables transmit data as light. They are high performance and expensive cables — they don't suffer interference and can transmit over very large distances at a high bandwidth without loss of signal quality.
- CAT 5e and CAT 6 are common types of Ethernet cable. They contain pairs of copper wires which are twisted together to reduce internal interference. They're cheaper than fibre optic cables and have a decent bandwidth, which is why they're commonly used in homes and offices to connect devices on a LAN.
- Coaxial cables are made of a single copper wire surrounded by a plastic layer for insulation and a metallic mesh which provides shielding from outside interference. They tend to be very cheap, although they also have a low bandwidth.

Twisted pair of copper wires
CAT 6 cable
Metallic mesh
Copper wire
Insulation
Coaxial cable

Wireless Networks use Radio Waves to transmit data

1) Local wireless networks are called WLANs (wireless LANs). Most people refer to these as Wi-Fi®, but Wi-Fi® is actually a specific family of WLAN protocols (see p61).

2) Like mobile phones and TVs, wireless networks use radio waves to transmit data.

3) To set up a wireless network, you need a Wireless Access Point (WAP) device. The WAP is basically a switch that allows devices to connect wirelessly.

4) Don't confuse WAPs with hotspots — locations where you can connect to a WAP.

5) To connect, devices need wireless capability. This is usually built-in these days, but if not you can use a USB dongle. HDMI dongles are popular for TVs.

Ralf and Rory chillaxing on a pair of dongles.

Wireless networks have benefits and drawbacks when compared to wired networks:

BENEFITS OF WIRELESS NETWORKS

1) Wireless networks are convenient, as you can get your device to automatically connect to the network, and can also move around while connected to the network.
2) They can be cheaper and better for the environment as you don't need any wires.
3) It's very easy to add more users to a wireless network — you don't need to install extra wires or do any complex setup.

DRAWBACKS OF WIRELESS NETWORKS

1) Wireless networks are generally less secure than wired networks — access points are usually visible to all devices, not just trusted ones, which can allow hackers to gain access.
2) Distance from the WAP, interference from other wireless networks, and physical obstructions (e.g. walls) can all reduce signal strength. This means there's a limit on how far a wireless network can reach.
3) They generally have a lower bandwidth and are less reliable than wired networks.

Hardware — nothing to do with concrete jackets...

In your exam, you might have to compare fibre optic and copper cables (which include CAT5e/6 and coaxial). You could also be asked which you think is more suited to a given situation. You should think in terms of cost (fibre optic = expensive, copper = cheap) and speed (fibre optic = fast, copper = slow).

Network Topologies

A topology is essentially the layout of the network. Networks can be arranged in lots of different topologies, but star and bus are the two important ones you'll need to know for the exam.

In a *Star* Topology all devices are connected to the centre

In a <u>star topology</u>, all the devices are connected to a <u>central switch</u> or <u>server</u> that controls the network.

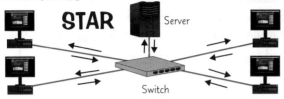

The central <u>switch</u> allows many devices to access the server simultaneously.

Star networks may be <u>wired</u> or <u>wireless</u>.

Pros
- If a <u>device fails</u> or a cable is disconnected, the rest of the network is <u>unaffected</u>.
- It's simple to <u>add more devices</u> to the network, since each device is connected to the switch using a <u>separate cable</u>.
- Star topologies tend to have <u>better performance</u> than other setups — data goes straight to the central device so all devices can <u>transmit data</u> at the <u>same time</u>.
- There are <u>very few data collisions</u> on a star network compared with other network topologies (e.g. bus).

Cons
- In <u>wired</u> networks, every device needs a <u>cable</u> to connect to the central switch or server. This can be <u>expensive</u>, e.g. for an office building with 50 terminals.
- The <u>switch</u> itself is also an <u>expensive</u> piece of hardware.
- If there is a <u>problem</u> with the switch or server then the <u>whole network</u> is affected.
- The <u>maximum</u> number of possible connections on the network is determined by the switch — if you need more, you might need to <u>buy a new one</u>.

In a *Bus* Topology all devices are connected to a *Single Cable*

1) <u>Bus topologies</u> use a single 'backbone' cable, called a <u>bus</u>, to connect all the devices.

2) Two <u>terminators</u> are placed at the <u>ends</u> of the bus to stop data ~~getting to Sarah Connor~~ <u>reflecting back</u> along the bus. Without the terminators, reflected signals would cause <u>interference</u> and potentially make the network <u>unusable</u>.

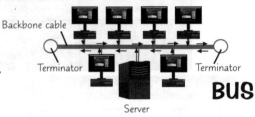

Pros
- Like in a star topology, the network is <u>unaffected</u> if a <u>device fails</u>.
- Bus networks aren't dependent on a <u>central switch</u> working to keep the whole network running.
- They're relatively <u>cheap</u> to set up compared to star networks. The <u>total length of wiring</u> needed is much less, and the <u>hardware</u> you need (the bus cable and terminators) is <u>cheaper</u> than switches, both to <u>buy</u> and to <u>maintain</u>.

Cons
- <u>Data collisions</u> are common on a bus network. When there is a data collision the data must be <u>resent</u>, which <u>slows</u> the network down.
- The <u>more devices</u> you add to the network, the <u>more likely</u> data collisions are. This makes bus topologies <u>unsuitable</u> for <u>large networks</u>.
- To try and avoid data collisions, devices must <u>wait</u> for the bus to be available before they can send any data — this can also <u>slow</u> the network down.
- If the bus cable gets <u>broken</u> (e.g. from nibbling rats), it <u>splits</u> the network into <u>separate parts</u>. Since the separated networks <u>don't have terminators</u> at <u>both ends</u> of the bus, there will be a lot of reflected signals which can <u>shut down</u> the <u>entire network</u>.

"You can't handle a bus network — you've got no backbone"...

Star networks are pretty common, but the fact that they rely on the central switch can cause all sorts of problems if the switch fails. Bus topologies are usually cheaper, but they can be really slow when there's heavy traffic — just like real buses. And if you'd like more driving similes, just keep reading.

Network Protocols

Moving data on the network is like going on a car journey — you need a destination, something to tell you how to get there, and rules to stop you crashing into anyone else on the road. That's where protocols come in.

Networks need Protocols to set the rules

1) A protocol is a set of rules for how devices communicate and how data is transmitted across a network.

2) Protocols cover how communication between two devices should start and end, how the data should be organised, and what the devices should do if data goes missing.

3) Data sent between networks is split into equal-sized packets. Each packet contains extra information like the destination and source addresses (see next page) and a checksum (used to find errors).

Network protocols are divided into Layers

to make the ultimate cake

1) A layer is a group of protocols which have similar functions.

2) Layers are self-contained — protocols in each layer do their job without needing to know what's happening in the other layers.

3) Each layer serves the layer above it — it does the hidden work needed for an action on the layer above. E.g. when you send an email (on layer 4), this triggers actions in layer 3, which triggers actions in layer 2, all the way down to layer 1.

> Data can only be passed between adjacent layers. E.g. Layer 2 can pass data to Layers 1 and 3 but Layer 1 can only pass data to Layer 2.

4) The four layers of the TCP/IP model are shown below:

	Layer Name	Protocols in this layer cover...	Protocol examples
icing	Layer 4 — Application Layer	Providing networking services to applications — e.g. turning data into websites.	HTTP, FTP, SMTP
avocado	Layer 3 — Transport Layer	Setting up communications between two devices, splitting data into packets and checking packets are correctly sent and delivered.	TCP, UDP
lemon	Layer 2 — Internet Layer	Adding IP addresses to data packets, directing them between devices and handling traffic. Used by routers.	IP
orange strawberry	Layer 1 — Link Layer	Passing data over the physical network. Responsible for how data is sent as electrical signals over cables, wireless and other hardware, e.g. NICs (p58), and for interpreting signals using device drivers (p53).	Wi-Fi®, Ethernet

ADVANTAGES OF USING LAYERS

1) It breaks network communication into manageable pieces. This helps developers concentrate on only one area of the network without having to worry about the others.

2) As layers are self-contained, they can be changed without the other layers being affected.

3) Having set rules for each layer forces companies to make compatible, universal hardware and software, so different brands will work with each other and always work in basically the same way.

Lots of Important Protocols work on the Application Layer

In the TCP/IP model, the application layer is responsible for things like file, email and data transfer:

Protocol	Stands for...	What is it used for?
HTTP	Hyper Text Transfer Protocol	Used by web browsers to access websites and communicate with web servers.
HTTPS	HTTP Secure	A more secure version of HTTP. Encrypts all information sent and received.
FTP	File Transfer Protocol	Used to access, edit and move files between devices on a network, e.g. to access files on a server from a client computer.
IMAP	Internet Message Access Protocol	Used to retrieve emails from a server.
SMTP	Simple Mail Transfer Protocol	Used to send emails. Also used to transfer emails between servers.

Protocols are like onions — they make me cry...

At least, I think that's why they're like onions. Anyway, there's lots of stuff to learn here — make sure you know what layers are, why they're useful and what all those different application layer protocols are for.

Network Protocols

TCP and UDP split the data into Packets

1) <u>TCP</u> and <u>UDP</u> are <u>transport layer</u> protocols which control the <u>packaging</u> and <u>unpackaging</u> of data.

2) <u>Transmission Control Protocol</u> (TCP) establishes a <u>connection</u> between the sending and receiving devices. It then splits the data into <u>numbered packets</u> that can be <u>reassembled</u> into the <u>original data</u> once they reach their destination, even if they arrive <u>out of order</u>.

3) It <u>communicates</u> with the receiving device to make sure that <u>all packets</u> have been <u>transferred correctly</u>. If not, the missing/corrupted packets can be <u>resent</u>. The sending device gets <u>confirmation</u> when the transfer is complete.

4) <u>User Datagram Protocol</u> (UDP) breaks the data down into packets <u>without numbering</u> them. They are <u>read</u> by the receiving device in the <u>order</u> that they <u>arrive</u> — even if that's not the order they were <u>sent</u>.

5) UDP only sends each packet <u>once</u> and <u>doesn't check</u> with the receiving device that everything has been <u>received</u>. This <u>saves time</u>, but there's <u>no way of knowing</u> if packets have gone <u>missing</u> in transit.

6) UDP is suitable for applications that need <u>fast</u>, <u>efficient</u> transmission, e.g. live video streaming. A hiccup in <u>video quality</u> from a missing packet is better than a <u>delay</u> in the live stream.

7) TCP is better when you need a <u>reliable</u> connection, e.g. downloading files. Missing data packets can cause files to be <u>corrupted</u> and <u>unusable</u>, but you wouldn't want to have to <u>redownload</u> the whole file.

IP is responsible for Packet Switching

1) <u>Internet Protocol</u> (IP) operates on the <u>Internet layer</u>, establishing <u>connections</u> between routers and handling <u>network traffic</u>. <u>IP addresses</u> are <u>unique</u> numbers assigned to <u>every device</u> connected to an IP network — they are added to the <u>header</u> of <u>each packet</u> at the Internet layer.

2) IP is responsible for <u>directing</u> data packets to their destination across the Internet or other IP networks using a process called <u>packet switching</u>.

3) Each packet is sent <u>between a series of routers</u> — each <u>router</u> reads the packet's header and uses the <u>IP address</u> to decide <u>which router</u> to send the packet to next.

He he he...

4) Which way the data is sent <u>changes</u> depending on network traffic — so the packets can take <u>different routes</u>. If a router receives too many packets at once, it may <u>prioritise</u> some over others.

5) Packet switching is an <u>efficient</u> use of the network because there are so many <u>possible routes</u> that each packet can take — packets can reach their receiving device quickly, even if there's <u>heavy traffic</u>.

Wi-Fi® is the Standard set of Protocols for Wireless LANs

1) Like we mentioned on p58, <u>Wi-Fi®</u> is a <u>family of protocols</u> commonly used in WLANs. It operates on the <u>link layer</u> — units of data sent on the link layer are called <u>frames</u> instead of packets.

2) Wi-Fi® uses two radio <u>frequency bands</u> — <u>2.4 GHz</u> and <u>5 GHz</u>. 2.4 GHz has a <u>greater range</u> and is better at <u>getting through walls</u> and other obstructions, while 5 GHz is <u>faster</u> over <u>short distances</u>.

Channels
1 2 3 4 5...

3) The bands are split into numbered <u>channels</u> that each cover a small frequency range. The channels in the 2.4 GHz band <u>overlap</u>. Networks using <u>adjacent</u> or <u>overlapping</u> channels can cause <u>interference</u>.

2.4 GHz   2.42 GHz   2.44 GHz

4) It's important that data is encrypted (see p64) on Wi-Fi® networks. There are <u>security protocols</u> for this, called <u>WPA™</u> (Wi-Fi® Protected Access) and <u>WPA2™</u>.

Wi-Fi® and Ethernet use switches to direct data frames to a device using its MAC address (p64).

ETHERNET IS USED ON WIRED NETWORKS

<u>Ethernet</u> is another <u>family of protocols</u> that operates on the <u>link layer</u>. Like Wi-Fi®, it also handles the transmission of data between devices on LANs, but Ethernet is specifically for <u>wired connections</u>.

I ended up with the wrong router — the packets were switched...

IP addresses usually look something like 37.153.62.136. They can be <u>static</u> (you get the same one every time you connect to a network) or <u>dynamic</u> (you can get a different one each time you connect to a network).

Cyber Security Threats

Networks are great for lots of reasons, but they can also cause a lot of headaches. Hackers and criminals are almost as imaginative as examiners when it comes to inflicting harm, so you need to take this stuff seriously.

Cyber Security is important to People and Organisations

1) Cyber security aims to protect networks, data, programs and computers against damage, cyber attacks and unauthorised access. It covers the technologies (e.g. anti-malware software), practices (e.g. network policies) and processes (e.g. penetration testing) used to do this.

2) Cyber attacks can target individuals, organisations or even governments. Hackers (see p69) often target organisations with the aim of accessing lots of sensitive information at once. There have been cases of millions of people's bank details being compromised by attacks on a single organisation.

Cyber attacks against governments or militaries, are sometimes called cyber warfare.

Penetration Testing can Test a system's Cyber Security

1) Penetration testing (or pentesting) is when organisations employ specialists to simulate potential attacks to their system. It's used to identify possible weaknesses in their cyber security. The results of the test are then reported back so that vulnerabilities can be fixed.

2) There are two different forms of penetration test — white box and black box.

- White box penetration testing simulates a malicious insider who has knowledge of the current system, e.g. an employee at the organisation. The person carrying out the test will be given user credentials to see what they can do with them.

- Black box penetration testing simulates an external cyber attack. The person carrying out the test will not be given any credentials, but will try to hack the organisation in any way they can.

Pen test
Fountain pen 7/10
Felt tip pen 5/10
Ball point pen /10

Malware is software that can harm devices

1) Malware (malicious software) is code that is designed to cause harm or gain unauthorised access to a computer system. It is often installed on someone's device without their knowledge or consent.

2) There are several different ways that malware can get onto a device — for example, being downloaded in an email attachment or hidden on removable media (e.g. USB drive or SD card).

2) Typical actions of malware include:

- Deleting or modifying files.
- Locking files — ransomware encrypts all the files on a computer. The user receives a message demanding a large sum of money be paid in exchange for a decryption key.
- Displaying unwanted adverts — adware can cause pop-up ads that cannot be closed.
- Monitoring the user — spyware secretly tracks actions like key presses and sends info to the hacker, who might be able to work out things like passwords and bank details.
- Altering permissions — rootkits can give hackers administrator-level access to devices.

3) Malware can spread between devices in different ways.

- Viruses attach (by copying themselves) to certain files, e.g. .exe files and autorun scripts. Users spread them by copying infected files and activate them by opening infected files.
- Worms are like viruses but they self-replicate without any user help, meaning they can spread very quickly. They exploit weaknesses in network security.
- Trojans are malware disguised as legitimate software. Unlike viruses and worms, trojans don't replicate themselves — users install them not realising they have a hidden purpose.

A worm got into my computer — I shouldn't leave it on the lawn...

You don't need to know every single type of malware out there, but learning all of the examples here will give you a great overview of how malware gets in and the chaos it can wreak once it's there.

Cyber Security Threats

Sci-fi movies might have lead you to believe that breaking into a network is all about tapping on a keyboard really quickly, but you'd be surprised how often it's done the old-fashioned way — manipulating people.

People are often the Weak Point in secure systems

Social engineering is a way of gaining sensitive information or illegal access to networks by influencing people, usually the employees of large companies. Social engineering comes in many different forms:

PHARMING

1) Pharming is where a user is directed to a fake version of a website (often a banking or shopping site), designed to look just like the real thing, with the aim that the user won't notice the difference.

2) When the user inputs their personal information into the website, they're actually handing it all over to the criminals, who can then access their genuine account.

3) Pharming is often carried out using malware that automatically redirects people from legitimate sites to fake ones. Ensuring that anti-malware software is up-to-date can reduce the risk of these attacks.

4) Internet browsers can use web filters to prevent users from accessing these fake sites.

PHISHING

1) Phishing is when criminals send emails or texts to people claiming to be from a well-known business, e.g. a bank or online retailer. The emails often lead the victim to a fake website, just like pharming.

2) Phishing emails are often sent to thousands of people, in the hope that someone will read the email and believe its content is legitimate.

3) Many email programs, browsers and firewalls have anti-phishing features that will reduce the number of phishing emails received. There are often giveaways that you can spot, e.g. poor grammar. Emails asking users to follow links or update personal details should always be treated with caution.

SHOULDERING

1) Shouldering is watching and observing a person's activity (typically over their shoulder).

2) Some examples of this are spying someone's PIN number at a cash machine, or watching someone putting their password into a secured computer.

3) It doesn't require any technical expertise or any planning. It's simple, but it can work. You can reduce risk by being discreet, e.g. covering the keypad when you enter your PIN.

That's right, type away...

Input my password? If you say so...

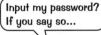

BLAGGING

1) Blagging is when someone makes up a story or pretends to be someone they're not, to persuade the victim to share information or do things they wouldn't normally do.

2) For example, a potential attacker could email someone, pretending to be one of their friends, saying they are stuck in a foreign country and need them to send money.

3) Another common method is to phone the victim, trying to gain their trust by persuading them that they are someone important — e.g. their boss's boss.

4) Criminals that use these tactics often try to pressure people, or rush them into giving away details without giving it proper thought. One way to reduce risk is to use security measures that can't be given away, e.g. biometrics (see p64).

The builders throw parties in the name of social engineering...

The best way to prevent social engineering in the workplace is to make employees aware of the dangers — this should be part of a company's network policy. The bottom line is: don't give away any details unless you're absolutely sure of who you're giving them to. Now, excuse me while I go answer my emails... — oh look, Derek needs me to send him £5000 to get home from Ibiza. Classic Derek...

Cyber Security Threats

Most organisations have a <u>network policy</u> — a set of rules and procedures that the organisation will follow to ensure their network is protected against any possible security threats, e.g. a cyber attack.

Networks need to be Protected against Threats

Organisations must keep their <u>networks secure</u> from <u>hackers</u> in order to protect sensitive information and comply with <u>data protection laws</u> (see p69). They can use several methods to help them do this:

Encryption is when data is translated into a code which only someone with the <u>correct key</u> can access, meaning unauthorised users cannot read it. Encrypted text is called <u>cipher text</u>, whereas data which has not been encrypted is called <u>plain text</u>. Encryption is essential for sending data over a network <u>securely</u>.

This book is encrypted.

The key is to stop reading it upside down.

Shut up malware!

Captain Firewall to the rescue!

Anti-malware software is designed to find and stop <u>malware</u> from damaging an organisation's network and the devices on it. There are lots of <u>different types</u> of anti-malware software. For example, <u>firewalls</u> examine <u>all data</u> entering and leaving a network and <u>block</u> any <u>potential threats</u>. Companies often use firewalls to <u>prevent unauthorised access</u> to their network.

Automatic software updates are used to <u>patch</u> (fix) any identified <u>security holes</u> in a piece of software. Software that is unpatched or outdated could be more easily <u>exploited</u> by hackers, malware and viruses.

User access levels control which parts of the network different groups of users can access. E.g. <u>business managers</u> are likely to have a <u>higher access level</u> allowing them to access <u>more sensitive data</u>, like pay information. User access levels <u>limit</u> the number of people with access to important data, so help to prevent attacks from <u>within</u> the organisation.

MAC address filtering is a way of making sure the only people on a <u>network</u> are <u>trusted users</u>. It checks the <u>unique identification</u> (MAC address) of each device that tries to connect to the network and only lets <u>allowed devices</u> join the network.

MAC addresses are unique identifiers assigned to network devices by the manufacturer — they can't be changed.

Authentication confirms your Identity

<u>User authentication</u> exists to make sure that <u>anyone</u> trying to access a network or use a system is who they say they are. This <u>prevents unauthorised people</u> from accessing data from the network.

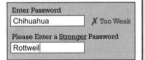

Enter Password
Chihuahua ✗ Too Weak
Please Enter a <u>Stronger</u> Password
Rottweil|

Passwords are a <u>simple</u> method of checking someone's identity. They should be strong — many characters long, use a <u>combination</u> of letters, numbers and symbols, and be <u>changed regularly</u>. Weak or default passwords are a big security risk.

Biometric measures use <u>scanners</u> to identify people by a unique part of their <u>body</u>, e.g. <u>fingerprint</u>, <u>retina</u>, etc. They have many different uses — for example, many <u>smartphones</u> now contain fingerprint scanners to <u>prevent unauthorised access</u>.

Email confirmation is used by most web services that require <u>account registration</u> to confirm that the <u>email address</u> belongs to the person registering. It is also used to stop people from using <u>fake</u> email addresses to <u>sign up</u> for things.

CAPTCHA stands for 'Completely Automated Public Turing test to tell Computers and Humans Apart' and is designed to <u>prevent programs</u> from <u>automatically</u> doing certain things, like <u>creating user accounts</u> on a website. It usually consists of a <u>simple task</u>, like typing out a <u>blurred</u> and <u>distorted word</u> from an image, or <u>recognising</u> things like animals and signposts.

Learn this page and your exam grade should be fairly secure...

You could be asked about threats or prevention, so make sure you know the last three pages really well. Heed Captain Firewall's wise words, ~~'die malware, just DIE!!!'~~ I mean 'preparation is key to success'.

Revision Questions for Section Six

From passwords to packets to PANs to protocols... you should now know petworks pinside pout.

- Try these questions and <u>tick off each one</u> when you <u>get it right</u>.
- When you've done <u>all the questions</u> for a topic and are <u>completely happy</u> with it, tick off the topic.

Networks, Hardware and Topologies (p57-59) ☑

1) What's the difference between a **LAN** and a **WAN**?

2) What type of network is Bluetooth® used for?

3) Give five benefits and four drawbacks of using a network.

4) What are the following devices used for? a) NICs b) switches c) routers

5) Describe three different types of network cable.

6) What type of network is commonly referred to as 'Wi-Fi®'?

7) Give two benefits and two drawbacks of using wireless networks over wired.

8) Give two advantages and two disadvantages of using a star network topology.

9) Describe the key features of a bus network topology.

Network Protocols (p60-61) ☑

10) What is the definition of a protocol?

11) List the 4 layers of the TCP/IP protocol model and the 4 layers of the ultimate cake.

12) Give three reasons why we divide protocols into layers.

13) What does each of the following stand for? Describe in a sentence what each one does:
       HTTP   HTTPS   FTP   IMAP   SMTP

14) Explain the differences between how TCP and UDP work.

15) Give one example of when you would use TCP, and one example of when you would use UDP.

16) Briefly describe how packet switching works.

17) Explain the difference between Wi-Fi® bands and Wi-Fi® channels.

18) What does WPA™ stand for and what does it do?

19) Name the family of protocols in charge of transmitting data over wired LANs.

Cyber Security Threats (p62-64) ☑

20) Give three reasons why someone might carry out a cyber attack.

21) Explain the difference between white box and black box penetration testing.

22) List five malicious actions that malicious software might maliciously carry out.

23) Describe three ways that malware can spread between devices.

24) What is meant by social engineering?

25) Give four social engineering methods, and say how you could reduce the risk of each.

26) Briefly describe five ways of protecting networks against threats.

27) What is user authentication?

28) Give three precautions you should take with your passwords.

29) My smartphone has a fingerprint scanner. What is the name for this kind of security measure?

30) Write down the two words in the image below. What kind of test is this and what does it prove?

fabric investigate

Ethical Issues

Despite what you might think, computer science doesn't just exist in a well-ventilated bubble — it affects all of our lives. Computers, new technology and the Internet all impact different people in different ways.

Issues created by technology come in Different Flavours

1) <u>Ethical</u> issues are about what would be considered <u>right</u> and <u>wrong</u> by society.
2) <u>Legal</u> issues are about what's actually <u>right</u> and <u>wrong</u> in the eyes of <u>the law</u>.
3) <u>Environmental</u> issues are about how we impact the natural world.

There is often <u>overlap</u> between ethical, legal and environmental issues.

Exam questions on issues could cover topics from earlier sections too, e.g. cloud storage (p52), wireless networks (p58) and cyber security (p62-64).

Digital Technology raises many Ethical Issues

As new digital technology becomes available, it can create a whole bunch of ethical issues.

1) <u>Smartphones</u> have allowed us to keep in touch much more easily, but have also allowed people to <u>neglect face-to-face interaction</u>. Some might say that it is making people <u>more rude</u> and <u>less sociable</u>.
2) <u>Wearable technology</u> has <u>many positive effects</u> — for example, <u>wireless headsets</u> may stop people from using their phone while driving and <u>fitness trackers</u> can help to promote healthy lifestyles. However, it can also cause problems. <u>Smart glasses</u> with built-in cameras have sparked controversy — people say the fact that they could be used to secretly photograph people is an <u>invasion of privacy</u>.
3) <u>Computer based implants</u> (chips that are surgically inserted into the body) may become more common in the future. They could allow better monitoring of our <u>health</u> and might make our daily lives more <u>convenient</u>, but will likely be <u>expensive</u> and may lead to <u>less privacy</u>.
4) Some people have <u>greater access</u> than others to these new digital technologies. People who have limited access to technology are at a heavy <u>disadvantage</u> — this is referred to as the <u>digital divide</u>.

> **CAUSES OF THE DIGITAL DIVIDE**
> - Some people don't have enough <u>money</u> to buy new devices like <u>smartphones</u> and <u>laptops</u>.
> - <u>Urban</u> areas may have better <u>network coverage</u> than <u>rural</u> areas.
> - Some people <u>don't know how</u> to use the Internet and other new technologies, and so are shut out of the opportunities they offer. This is a problem for many <u>older people</u> who haven't grown up with computers and so have little experience with them.

5) The <u>global divide</u> is created by the fact that the level of access to technology is different in different <u>countries</u>. People in richer countries tend to have greater access to technology than people in poorer countries. The Internet and other technologies have created lots of opportunities for the people with access to them, so this has <u>increased</u> the inequality between poorer and richer countries.

Probably the most issue-ful technology is The Internet

1) The Internet gives people greater <u>anonymity</u>, which can enable <u>anti-social</u> and <u>abusive</u> behaviour:

- <u>Cyberbullying</u> is when somebody uses the Internet to deliberately <u>intimidate</u>, <u>insult</u> or <u>humiliate</u> someone. It can cause serious <u>distress</u> — people have been driven to <u>suicide</u> because of these attacks.
- <u>Trolling</u> is when somebody tries to cause <u>public arguments</u> with others online, only making comments which <u>frustrate</u> other people. Trolls normally do this for their own <u>amusement</u> or to gain <u>attention</u>.

2) People now use the Internet for things they'd traditionally do in person, e.g. <u>online banking</u> and <u>shopping</u>. This means that organisations now store a lot of our <u>personal data</u> — they have an ethical (and legal) responsibility to have <u>good cyber security</u> (see p62) to prevent things like <u>identity theft</u>.
3) This is also true of companies providing the public with <u>wireless access</u> to the Internet (e.g. cafes that offer free Wi-Fi®). Many would argue that they also have a responsibility to <u>restrict access</u> to certain websites (such as gambling and pornography sites), as <u>children</u> could be able to gain access.

If you've got an issue, here's a high-tech nose-blowing device...

Exam questions may ask you to talk about ethical, legal <u>and</u> environmental issues, rather than just one. The more points you can make, the better — just make sure all your points are relevant to the question.

Ethical Issues

Computers have had a tremendous impact on society — it's difficult to imagine some of the things we do today without them. Just remember that this technological revolution is not always smiles and rainbows...

Technology is changing how we Access Services

New technology has provided new ways for people to obtain goods and services, although these modern conveniences can create lots of ethical issues.

1) The ability to wirelessly stream music and television has allowed customers to access media conveniently and cheaply, either for free or through a subscription service. But users of these services often don't own what they're paying for, and they can lose access if their subscription ends or if the service closes down.

2) The rise in popularity of smartphones has lead to certain apps becoming very successful — for example, the Uber app lets you turn your car into a taxi service.

3) These services are often cheap and convenient, but they draw customers away from traditional businesses (e.g. taxi companies). Also, they may be more risky for customers as they are not necessarily regulated as strictly as traditional businesses are.

4) There are also many computing services that are now offered for free — cloud storage (p52) and webmail are examples of this. Often, these services will have limits on what you can access for free, and a superior 'premium' service that costs money. This could help to reduce the digital divide by providing partial services to people who otherwise couldn't afford them.

> This is sometimes called a 'freemium' model.

5) This type of business model can also been seen in mobile games — however, some say that these games exploit people with more impulsive spending habits. There have also been cases of parents accidentally allowing their children to spend hundreds of pounds on these games.

Technology is also changing How Businesses Operate

1) A lot of businesses expect people to be able to use technology and access services online. For example, employers may expect people to be able to apply for jobs online, and many require employees to have at least some basic computer skills. However, some people may not have access to technology for various reasons (see p66), which puts them at an unfair disadvantage.

2) The popularity of mobile devices has lead to some businesses insisting that employees carry a smartphone with them all the time, so that they can always be contacted, either by phone or by email. This can be stressful for employees who feel they can never really switch off from work.

3) In fact, some companies have taken this one step further and have offered their employees computer chip implants (see previous page) that are used to open security doors and access their computer. This is far more secure than traditional password or keycard systems, but many people find the idea of implanting technology in humans to be unethical.

4) Marketing and advertising have also been greatly affected by new technology. Pop-ups appear all over the Internet and targeted adverts are shown to people on social media sites. This has lead to people feeling swamped by advertising online, and has made programs like AdBlock popular. However, lots of free services are funded by advertising money, so if everybody blocked the adverts, then the providers of these services would lose their income and may have to start charging for the service instead.

5) Even though businesses can take advantage of technology in lots of ways, they have to be careful — if they ignored the ethical impact of their actions, even if they were legal, they could lose public trust. Many businesses have a code of conduct (a set of rules that the business and its employees will follow) to show the public that they take these ethical issues seriously.

Don't mind grumpy over there — he's got a chip in his shoulder...

New technology isn't always a good thing, but look at the bright side: there's a good chance it'll be replaced by the next big thing in a few years' time anyway. Who knows — maybe one day, paper books like this one will be relics of the ancient past... Anyway, remember in the exam that businesses are big users and developers of technology, but they don't always have everyone's best interest at heart.

Ethical Issues

It's quite concerning to think how many people actually saw your last social media status. Guess we should count ourselves lucky though — some people in the world don't get to access social media at all.

It's hard to keep information Private on the Internet

1) Most people generally want to be able to keep their personal information <u>private</u>. However, this rarely happens in practice, as many online services require you to provide your details in order to use them. For example:
   - Many websites (shopping, banking, etc.) require users to provide <u>personal information</u> in order to set up an account, e.g. date of birth and address.
   - <u>Social media</u> websites actively <u>encourage</u> you to post even more personal information, including photographs and details of your job and social life.

2) Users will accept a <u>privacy agreement</u> before using many websites and software. The trouble is that very few people actually read these, so most are <u>unaware</u> of what they're agreeing to. Even if they <u>do</u> read the terms, users often have <u>no choice</u> but to agree if they want to use the website or software at all.

3) Companies can do lots of things with your details as long as they stay <u>within the bounds</u> of the privacy agreement. They can make your information available to <u>other people</u>, or <u>sell</u> your <u>personal details</u>, <u>buying habits</u> etc. to other organisations (who could use it to send you <u>targeted adverts</u> or <u>spam</u> emails).

4) Users can take steps to make the information they share more <u>private</u>, e.g. change their <u>privacy settings</u> on social media sites (which are often fairly relaxed by <u>default</u>).

5) Users have to trust companies to keep their data <u>secure</u>. But this doesn't always happen — there have been various <u>high profile cases</u> where customer data held by large companies has been <u>leaked</u> or <u>stolen</u>.

Surveillance and Censorship are controversial issues

1) <u>Computer surveillance</u> is when someone <u>monitors</u> what other people are accessing on the Internet.

2) Many countries use some form of surveillance. Government <u>security services</u> may use packet sniffers and other software to <u>monitor Internet traffic</u>, looking out for certain <u>key words</u> or <u>phrases</u> that might alert them to illegal activities, terrorism, etc. Often, governments will push for <u>greater powers</u> (e.g. access to private emails) to assist in catching criminals, but might face <u>opposition</u> from the public.

3) In some countries, <u>Internet Service Providers</u> (ISPs) <u>keep records</u> of all websites visited by all its customers for a certain amount of time, and may be <u>legally required</u> to share data with <u>security services</u>.

4) <u>Internet censorship</u> is when someone tries to <u>control</u> what other people can access on the Internet. Some countries' governments use censorship to restrict access to certain information.

5) One of the strictest countries for censorship is <u>China</u>, where they restrict access to websites which are <u>critical</u> of the government. China also censors many major <u>foreign websites</u>, including Facebook®, YouTube™ and Twitter. In <u>Cuba</u>, citizens can only access the Internet from government-controlled <u>access points</u>.

6) Many governments use <u>some form</u> of censorship. Many countries (including the UK) restrict access to pornography, gambling and other inappropriate websites in order to <u>protect children</u>.

7) Censorship and surveillance are <u>controversial</u> topics. Some people support them in some form, e.g. to protect children or to stop terrorism. Others are completely against them, including several non-profit organisations which campaign against what they call <u>cyber censorship</u> and <u>mass surveillance</u>.

** This content has been removed to protect you from bad jokes...**

Do you ever get the feeling you're being watched? No? Just me then. The weird thing about the stuff on this page is that everyone knows it's happening but no-one does anything about it — the Internet is such a big part of modern life that for many people their loss of privacy is a price worth paying. Other people aren't so keen about losing their privacy though, which I guess is why these issues are so controversial.

Legal Issues

Since computers went mainstream, the law has had to keep up with the way people use and abuse them. The Internet causes lots of issues, since it's so difficult to police what people do online.

Laws Control the use of your Personal Data

1) When an organisation stores someone's personal data on their system, that person is entitled to certain rights, stated in data protection laws. These rights can be summarised by the principles shown here.

2) Before collecting personal data, an organisation must register with the government, saying what data they'll collect, and how they'll use it.

3) Organisations have a legal obligation to have good cyber security (p62) on their networks to keep personal data secure. This can be hard for small businesses, who may not be able to afford top-of-the-range security software.

4) Companies using cloud storage (see p52) to store personal data must ensure that the service is trustworthy and reliable. They should also understand how and where the data is being stored, especially when servers in other countries are used.

Data must only be used in a fair and lawful way.	Data must only be used for the specified purpose.	Data should be adequate, relevant and not excessive for the specified use.
Data should not be transferred abroad without adequate protection.	**Data Protection Principles**	Data must be accurate and kept up to date.
Data should be kept safe and secure.	The rights of the individual must be observed.	Data should not be kept longer than is necessary.

The Computer Misuse Act prevents illegal access to files

The Computer Misuse Act was introduced to stop hacking and cyber crime (see below). It introduced three new offences:

How do you like my new smartwatch?

The long arm of the law.

1) Gaining unauthorised access to a private network or device, e.g. through hacking (just accessing a network could get you a fine or prison sentence).

2) Gaining unauthorised access to a network or device in order to commit a crime, like stealing data or destroying the network.

3) Unauthorised modification of computer material — e.g. deleting or changing files. The Act also makes it illegal to make, supply or obtain malware.

Cyber Crime is a major problem

1) Cyber crime refers to any illegal activity that involves computers. The most infamous type of cyber criminal are hackers.

> Hacking refers to gaining access to a system by exploiting weaknesses in its security. This is usually done to steal or destroy data, or to infect the system with malware (p62). However, some companies employ 'good' hackers to identify vulnerabilities through penetration testing (p62).

2) There are lots of different methods that hackers use to attack systems, including:
   - passive attacks — monitoring data on a network, e.g. using packet sniffer software.
   - active attacks — using malware or other means to attack a system directly.
   - brute force attacks — using automated software and trial-and-error to crack passwords.
   - denial-of-service attacks — preventing people from using a network by flooding it with useless traffic.

3) Since cyber criminals tend to have a good understanding of networks and security measures, they often know how to avoid being tracked down, making it very difficult to catch and prosecute them.

Hacking is computer misuse, so stop chopping up your laptop...

Make sure that you understand what hacking is all about (that's not an invitation to try it out, though). You don't need to memorise all of the data protection principles given above, but the more you know about it, the more points you'll be able to make in the exam. And that's why we're here, right?

Legal Issues

Another important legal area is intellectual property — stuff people create. When it comes to computers, intellectual property often involves things like hardware, software, computer code and algorithms.

Copyright and Patents protect innovation

1) The Copyright, Designs and Patents Act protects intellectual property (anything someone has created, e.g. a novel, a song, software, a new invention) from being copied or stolen by other people.

2) Patents cover new inventions — they protect ideas and concepts rather than actual content. Normally, you have to apply for (and pay for) a patent. In computing, patents mostly apply to pieces of hardware.

3) Copyright covers written or recorded content, e.g. books, music, and films. Copyright usually applies to works without needing to apply for it. The Act makes it illegal to share copyrighted material without the copyright holder's permission, or to plagiarise (copy) somebody else's work.

   - Most software is protected by copyright. It's illegal to use or share a piece of copyrighted software without a license. Some developers choose to make their software open source (see below).
   - Computer code is usually copyright protected, although it's hard to protect smaller pieces of code.
   - Algorithms (e.g. bubble sort) tend to not be copyright protected. In certain countries, developers are able to get patents for more specific algorithms (e.g. filtering algorithms used in search engines).

5) It can be difficult to prove that computer code has been copied, because:

   - Similarities in code may just be down to coincidence, particularly if both programs were written to perform the same task. It is very difficult to measure how 'original' a piece of code is.
   - Creators of paid software will often want to keep their source code secret to prevent competitors from seeing and copying it. However, not being able to directly compare the source code makes it hard to identify where code has been copied.

6) The Internet has made it harder to protect copyrighted content due to the ease of file sharing. Developers often include DRM (digital rights management) with software — this attempts to prevent unauthorised use of software with things like activation keys and online authentication.

7) Software with DRM is a common target of cracking. Cracking is where users illegally modify the software to remove or bypass unwanted features.

8) Cracked software is often distributed online, which leads people to argue that DRM doesn't work and that it only inconveniences legitimate users. Some DRM can even make older software unusable if the authentication service is no longer available.

9) As well as being illegal, using cracked software can lead to a loss of income for the software creator. This could discourage them from fixing bugs in the software or developing new software. Hackers also often use cracked software to distribute malware, e.g. by including a virus (see p62).

Some content can be Copied and Shared Legally

1) There is a lot of open source software available online, where users are allowed to freely download and modify the source code (see p29). Well-known examples include Apache HTTP Server™ (runs web servers), GIMP (image editing), Mozilla® Firefox® (web browser), and VLC media player (it's a ...).

2) Open source software is often distributed using Creative Commons (CC) licences. These allow users to legally share the software, while specifically allowing and disallowing certain actions (e.g. modifying the code, using it for profit, etc.).

3) Popular open source software is often supported by a strong online community, where people work together to improve the software and fix bugs.

I just bought Einstein's house — it's my intellectual property...

There are loads of points you can make about these issues. Getting the difference between copyright and patents right can be particularly tricky — remember that copyright protects real stuff that has been written and covers software, while patents protect concepts and are mostly relevant to hardware.

Environmental Issues

Devices have a huge environmental impact. Take a smartphone — it's made of materials that have to be mined from the Earth, when it's used it consumes energy, and when it's thrown away it could end up on a landfill site.

When we *Make devices* we use up *Natural Resources*

1) Electronic devices contain lots of <u>raw materials</u>.

2) <u>Plastics</u> (which are used for casing and other parts) come from <u>crude oil</u>.

3) Devices also contain many <u>precious metals</u> like gold, silver, copper, mercury, palladium, platinum, indium and fancyshinyinium*. Many of these metals only occur naturally in <u>tiny quantities</u>.

4) Extracting these materials uses lots of <u>energy</u>, creates <u>pollution</u> and depletes scarce <u>natural resources</u>.

When we *Use devices* we use *Energy... lots of it*

All the billions of devices in the world today are consuming energy in the form of <u>electricity</u> — a lot of it.

1) Most electricity is made using <u>non-renewable</u> resources like coal, oil and gas. <u>Extracting</u> these resources and <u>producing electricity</u> in power stations causes lots of <u>pollution</u> including greenhouse gases.

2) All computers generate <u>heat</u> and require cooling. The powerful <u>servers</u> used by businesses and the Internet are a particular problem. They're very <u>power hungry</u> and require special <u>air-conditioned</u> rooms to keep them cool. That means using even more energy and more pollution.

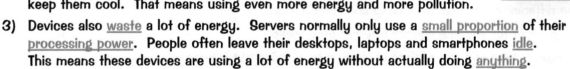

One for me and one for you.

3) Devices also <u>waste</u> a lot of energy. Servers normally only use a <u>small proportion</u> of their <u>processing power</u>. People often leave their desktops, laptops and smartphones <u>idle</u>. This means these devices are using a lot of energy without actually doing <u>anything</u>.

4) There are several ways to <u>reduce</u> the amount of energy wasted by devices:

- <u>Virtual servers</u> are <u>software-based</u> servers rather than real machines. Multiple virtual servers can run on one physical server, so the physical server can run at <u>full capacity</u>.
- <u>Switching off</u> mobile devices <u>overnight</u>, or putting them into <u>sleep</u> mode, can save power.
- Devices often use more energy when searching for a <u>wireless</u> connection. Disabling this, or using a <u>wired</u> connection, could preserve battery life.

When we *Throw Away devices* we create loads of *E-waste*

1) <u>E-waste</u> is a huge problem — the world creates <u>20-50 million tonnes</u> of e-waste every year. Modern devices have a very <u>short life</u> before they're discarded — either because they <u>break</u> or because people want to <u>upgrade</u> (particularly with smartphones).

2) <u>Device manufacturers</u> and <u>retailers</u> are part of this problem. They provide short <u>warranties</u> (e.g. 1 year), use <u>marketing</u> to convince people to upgrade and have pricing policies that make it <u>cheaper to replace</u> than to repair.

3) The Waste Electric and Electronic Equipment (<u>WEEE</u>) directive was created to tackle the e-waste problem. The WEEE has rules for disposing of e-waste <u>safely</u>, to promote <u>reuse</u> (e.g. refurbishing broken devices to use again) and <u>recycling</u> (e.g. extracting the devices' <u>precious metals</u>).

4) To <u>cut costs</u> a lot of e-waste is sent to certain African and Asian countries where regulations are less strict. Here, most of it ends up in <u>landfill</u> and can be a hazard — toxic chemicals can leak into the <u>ground water</u> and harm wildlife.

Don't (e-)waste your time — use your energy to learn this page...

I know this sounds very negative, but it's not all bad news — the Internet lets us talk to each other without having to travel long distances in pollution-spouting vehicles, cloud storage has reduced the need for things like CDs, and wireless networking means fewer resources are wasted on cables. *OK, that one may be made up...*

Revision Questions for Section Seven

Well, that section had a lot of issues — thankfully you're not here to solve its problems, just learn its content.

- Try these questions and <u>tick off each one</u> when you <u>get it right</u>.
- When you've done <u>all the questions</u> for a topic and are <u>completely happy</u> with it, tick off the topic.

Ethical Issues (p66-68) ☑

1) Define each type of issue in a sentence: a) ethical   b) legal   c) environmental ☑
2) Give one positive and one negative ethical issue caused by:
   a) mobile devices   b) wearable technology   c) the Internet ☑
3) Give three reasons why a digital divide exists. ☑
4) What is: a) cyberbullying?   b) trolling? ☑
5) Give a reason why cyberbullying and trolling have become so common. ☑
6) Give three examples of services that have been changed by new technology. ☑
7) Explain, in 30 words or less, how businesses can be affected by each of the following:
   a) mobile devices   b) the Internet   c) computer-based implants ☑
8) Give two reasons why someone might give their personal details to a website. ☑
9) Give two problems with many online companies' privacy agreements. ☑
10) What can you do to make the information you share online more private? ☑
11) Explain the difference between censorship and surveillance. ☑
12) Give one argument for and one against Internet censorship. ☑
13) Give one argument for and one against governments carrying out Internet surveillance. ☑

Legal Issues (p69-70) ☑

14) a) When do data protection laws apply?
    b) Give three data protection principles. ☑
15) What three offences does the Computer Misuse Act cover? ☑
16) a) What is a hacker?
    b) Describe four methods that a hacker might use to attack a system. ☑
17) Define: a) intellectual property   b) patents   c) copyright ☑
18) Explain how copyright and patents apply to:
    a) software   b) computer code   c) algorithms ☑
19) Describe two reasons why someone may find it difficult to prove if their code has been copied. ☑
20) a) What does DRM stand for? What is it used for?
    b) What is meant by cracking? ☑
21) What is meant by 'open source' software? Give two examples. ☑
22) Why might a software developer want to use a Creative Commons licence? ☑

Environmental Issues (p71) ☑

23) Give three examples of natural resources which are used to make computers. ☑
24) Explain how a device's need for energy impacts the environment. ☑
25) Give three ways to reduce the amount of energy devices waste. ☑
26) What is e-waste and why do we generate a lot of it? ☑
27) Describe an environmental danger caused by e-waste left in landfill sites. ☑

Answers

Below are answers to a handful of end of section <u>revision questions</u>. The answers to all of the other revision questions can be found by looking back over the section.

Page 7 — Section One

Q8 E.g.

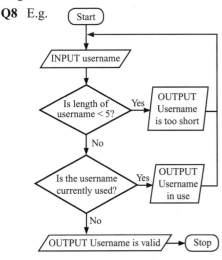

Q11 a) <u>Binary Search:</u>
The middle item is the 4th item, *Dagenham,* which comes before *Morpeth.*
So <u>lose first half of list</u> to leave: *Morpeth, Usk, Watford*
The middle item of the new list is the 2nd item, *Usk,* which comes after *Morpeth* so <u>lose second half of list</u> to leave: *Morpeth*
The middle item of the new list is the 1st item, which is *Morpeth,* so you've found the correct item.

Even when there is one entry left you still have to carry on with the algorithm to check that it is the correct entry.

b) <u>Linear Search:</u>
Ashington ≠ Morpeth
Brecon ≠ Morpeth
Chester ≠ Morpeth
Dagenham ≠ Morpeth
Morpeth = Morpeth
You've found the correct item.

Q13 b) **1st pass (4 swaps):**
<u>O, B</u>, A, P, G, L
B, <u>O, A</u>, P, G, L
B, A, O, <u>P, G</u>, L
B, A, O, G, <u>P, L</u>
B, A, O, G, L, P
2nd pass (3 swaps):
<u>B, A</u>, O, G, L, P
A, B, <u>O, G</u>, L, P
A, B, G, <u>O, L</u>, P
A, B, G, L, O, P
3rd pass (no swaps):
A, B, G, L, O, P

Q15 a)

8	7	5	1	3	6	4	2

8	7	5	1		3	6	4	2

8	7		5	1		3	6		4	2

8		7		5	1		3		6		4		2

7	8		1	5		3	6		2	4

1	5	7	8		2	3	4	6

1	2	3	4	5	6	7	8

b) **1st pass (4 swaps):**
8 7 5 <u>1 3</u> 6 4 2
8 7 5 3 <u>1 6</u> 4 2
8 7 5 3 6 <u>1 4</u> 2
8 7 5 3 6 4 <u>1 2</u>
8 7 5 3 6 4 2 1
2nd pass (2 swaps):
8 7 5 <u>3 6</u> 4 2 1
8 7 5 6 <u>3 4</u> 2 1
8 7 5 6 4 3 2 1
3rd pass (1 swap):
8 7 <u>5 6</u> 4 3 2 1
8 7 6 5 4 3 2 1
4th pass (no swaps):
8 7 6 5 4 3 2 1

Page 24 — Section Two

Q2 a) STRING_TO_INT('1234')
b) REAL_TO_STRING(0.578)
c) INT_TO_STRING(8)
d) STRING_TO_REAL('0.75')

Q5 b) (i) 7 (ii) 2 (iii) 'mage'

Q9 first_day ← USERINPUT
IF first_day = 'Sunday'
OR first_day = 'Monday' THEN
   OUTPUT 5
ELSE
   OUTPUT 4
ENDIF

Q10 FOR i ← 1 TO 100
   roll ← RANDOM_INT(1, 8)
   OUTPUT roll
ENDFOR

Q12 a) OUTPUT chars[4]
b) chars[2] ← 'D'
c) FOR i ← 0 to 9
   chars[i] ← 'N'
ENDFOR

Q13 FOR i ← 0 TO 9
   FOR j ← 0 TO 9
      multiply[i][j] ← i * j
   ENDFOR
ENDFOR

Page 30 — Section Three

Q9 Range check — the program checks if the user has entered a year between 1900 and 2016 before breaking out of the REPEAT-UNTIL loop.

Q13 For example:
- Normal input data (e.g. 'art')
- No input (e.g. ' ')
- A string with no anagram (e.g. 'x')
- Mixed case string (e.g. 'aRT')
- Other characters (e.g. 2?#)

Q15

x	arr[x]	total
		1
0	2	2
1	5	10
2	1	10
3	2	20
4	3	60

Page 45 — Section Four

Q2

A	B	C	A OR B	(A OR B) AND C
0	0	0	0	0
0	0	1	0	0
0	1	0	1	0
0	1	1	1	1
1	0	0	1	0
1	0	1	1	1
1	1	0	1	0
1	1	1	1	1

Q5 a) 0.2 gigabytes
b) 1 600 000 000 bits

Q6 10001111

Q8 a) (i) 10001 (ii) 10010100
    (iii) 11110000
b) (i) 11 (ii) 94 (iii) F0

Q9 a) (i) 56 (ii) 159 (iii) 43
b) (i) 38 (ii) 9F (iii) 2B

Q10 a) (i) 74 (ii) 117 (iii) 3033
b) (i) 1001010 (ii) 1110101
    (iii) 101111011001

Q22 a) (4, P), (2, Q), (3, R),
    (6, S), (5, P), (3, Q)

b)

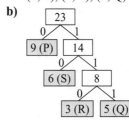

c) (i) 23 × 8 = 184 bits.
(ii) The number of bits needed for each character using the Huffman coding is shown in the table below:

Char.	Code	Freq.	Bits
P	0	9	9
Q	111	5	15
R	110	3	9
S	10	6	12

This gives a total of
9 + 15 + 9 + 12 = 45 bits.
(iii) 8 × 2 × 6 = 96 bits

Glossary and Index

Glossary and Index

Glossary and Index

H

hacker A person who tries to access or attack a computer network or device by exploiting weaknesses in its security. **69**

hard disk drive (HDD) Traditional internal storage for PCs and laptops that stores data magnetically. **46, 51**

hardware The physical parts of a computer system. **46, 53, 58**

heat sink Pulls heat away from the CPU to help maintain its temperature. **46**

hexadecimal A counting system using base-16 consisting of the digits 0-9 and the letters A-F. **37, 38**
   converting to/from binary 38
   converting to/from decimal 37

high-level language A programming language like C++ and Java™ that is easy for humans to understand. **29**

hotspot A location where people can access a wireless access point. **58**

HTTP (Hyper Text Transfer Protocol) Used by web browsers to access websites and communicate with web servers. **60**

HTTPS (HTTP Secure) A version of HTTP that encrypts data. **60**

Huffman coding A type of lossless compression that assigns codes of varying length to data based on its frequency. **44**

I

IF statement A type of selection statement. **12**

image resolution The number of pixels in an image. **40**

IMAP (Internet Message Access Protocol) A protocol used to retrieve emails from a server. **60**

indefinite iteration A type of iteration statement where the number of times it repeats depends on a condition. **14**

indentation Spaces put at the beginning of lines of code to help show a program's structure. **25**

input validation Checking that an input meets certain criteria. **26**

integer (data type) A numerical data type for whole numbers. **8**

intellectual property An original piece of work (or an idea) that someone has created and belongs to them. **70**

Internet The ultimate / biggest / best WAN in the world, based around the TCP/IP protocol. **57**

Internet layer One of the layers in the TCP/IP network protocol model. **60, 61**

Internet Protocol (IP) The protocol responsible for packet switching. **61**

interpreter A translator that turns source code into machine code and runs it one instruction at a time. **29**

I/O (input/output) device 53

IP address A unique identifier given to a device when it accesses an IP network. **61**

iteration statement A statement which makes the program repeat a set of instructions. **14, 15**

K

kilobyte 1000 bytes. **33**

L

LAN (Local Area Network) A network which only covers a single site. **57**

layers (network) Groups of protocols that have similar functions. **60**

legal issue An issue relating to what's right and wrong in the eyes of the law. **66, 69, 70**

linear search algorithm 4

link layer One of the layers in the TCP/IP network protocol model. **60, 61**

local variable A variable that is only defined and usable within certain parts of a program. **23**

logic circuit An electronic circuit for performing logic operations on binary data. It may have more than one logic gate and more than two inputs. **32**

logic error When a program does something that was not intended. **27**

logic gate An electronic circuit component that performs a Boolean operation (e.g. AND, OR or NOT). **31**

loop (programming) A set of instructions that the program repeats until a condition is met or count is reached. **14, 15**

lossless compression Temporarily removing data from a file to decrease the file size. **42**

lossy compression Permanently removing data from the file to decrease the file size. **42**

low-level language A programming language that is close to what a CPU would actually do and is written for specific hardware (i.e. CPU type). E.g. machine code and assembly languages. **29**

M

MAC address A unique identifier assigned to a device that cannot be changed. **64**

MAC address filtering A way of keeping networks secure by blocking devices from accessing the network unless their unique identification (MAC address) is known and trusted. **64**

machine code The lowest-level programming language consisting of 0s and 1s. CPUs can directly process it as a string of CPU instructions. **29**

magnetic storage Hard disk drives and magnetic tapes that hold data as magnetised patterns. **51**

mainframe (or supercomputer) An extremely powerful (and expensive and reliable) computer for specialist applications. **46**

malware Malicious software created to damage or gain illegal access to computer systems. **62, 64**

megabyte 1000 kilobytes. **33**

memory Hardware used to store data that a CPU needs access to. **48, 49, 54**

merge sort algorithm 6

module (structured programming) Each independent part of a program after decomposition. **25**

motherboard The main circuit board in a computer that other hardware connects to. **46, 49**

Mr Floppy 52

multitasking (OS) When an operating system runs multiple programs and applications at the same time. **53, 54**

N

nested statement A selection or iteration statement made up of multiple statements inside each other. **12, 15**

network interface card (NIC) An internal piece of hardware that allows a device to connect to a network. **58**

network policy A set of rules and procedures an organisation will follow to ensure their network is protected against attacks. **64**

network security Protection against network attacks. **64**

nibble 4 bits. **33**

non-volatile memory Memory that retains its contents when it has no power. **49**

normal data Test data that simulates the inputs that users are likely to enter. **27**

NOT One of the Boolean operators.
   logic gate 31
   operator 16

Glossary and Index

Glossary and Index

string A data type for text.
    data type 8
    manipulation 11

structured programming A programming technique which breaks down the main program into small manageable modules. **25**

subroutine A set of code within a program that can be called at any time from the main program. **22, 23**

surveillance The act of monitoring what people are accessing on the Internet. **68**

switch (network) Connects devices together on a LAN. **58**

syntax error An error in the code where the rules or grammar of the programming language have been broken. **27**

system cleanup utility A piece of system software that finds and removes files that are no longer in use. **55**

system software Software designed to run or maintain a computer system. **46, 53-55**

T

TCP (Transmission Control Protocol) A transport layer protocol that communicates with the recipient to ensure all data is sent correctly. **61**

TCP/IP model A network protocol model that separates protocols into four layers. **60**

terabyte 1000 gigabytes. **33**

terminator A piece of hardware used on a bus network that prevents data from bouncing back along the bus. **59**

tertiary storage High-capacity external storage used mainly for backups. **51**

test data Inputs that are chosen to see if a program is behaving as intended. **27**

testing A way of checking if a program functions correctly. **27**

test plan A detailed plan of how a program is going to be tested, including what test data will be used. **27**

time efficiency A measure of how 'quickly' an algorithm completes a task. **28**

topology (networks) How the devices in a network are connected together. **59**

trace table A table that keeps track of the value of certain variables as a program is run. **28**

traffic (networks) The amount of data travelling on a network. **61**

translator A program that turns a programming language into machine code. **29**

transport layer One of the layers in the TCP/IP network protocol model. **60, 61**

trojans A type of malware which is disguised as legitimate software. **62**

trolling The act of trying to provoke public arguments online. **66**

truth table A table listing all possible binary inputs through a logic circuit, with the corresponding outputs. **31, 32**

typical data Test data that simulates the inputs that users are likely to enter. **27**

U

UDP (User Datagram Protocol) A transport layer protocol that sends packets quickly without checking whether or not they are received. **61**

Unicode® A large character set that attempts to include all possible characters. **39**

units (of data) 33

user access levels Controls what files or areas of the network different groups of users can access. **64**

user account 54

user interface Provides a way for the user to interact with the computer. **53**

utility software Software designed to help maintain a computer system. **55**

V

validation Checking that an input meets certain criteria. **26**

variable A named value which can be changed as the program is running. **10**
    local / global 23

virtual server A software-based server. **71**

virus A type of malware which spreads by attaching itself to files. **62**

virus scanner A piece of system software that checks a computer for potential threats. **55**

volatile memory Memory that loses its contents when it has no power. **49**

Von Neumann A type of CPU architecture. **48**

W

WAN (Wide Area Network) A network which connects networks in different geographical locations. **57**

Waste Electric and Electronic Equipment (WEEE) directive 71

well-maintained code Code that is easy for other programmers to understand and change. **25**

WHILE loop A type of indefinite iteration statement. **14**

white box penetration testing A form of penetration testing where the tester is given system credentials. Used to simulate a cyber attack from within the organisation. **62**

Wi-Fi® The standard family of protocols used for WLANs. **58, 61**

WIMP A user interface based on windows, icons, menus and pointers. **53**

wired / wireless networks 57, 58

wireless access point (WAP) A piece of hardware that allows devices to connect wirelessly. **58**

WLAN (Wireless Local Area Network) A LAN that uses wireless technology to transmit data between devices. **58**

worms A type of malware which replicates itself. **62**